100 Quick & Easy Crochet Stitches™

Table of Contents

Introduction

HOW TO CUT YOUR CROCHET TIME UP TO 50 PERCENT OR MORE!

Who doesn't want to learn how to crochet faster than ever? Pick any of the 100 patterns featured in this book to get started. None of the patterns are complicated and consist of mostly double crochet stitches and chains to work up quickly—most are easy to memorize. But there are ways you can crochet faster. These tricks will help you make a last-minute project in much less time—just the ticket when you've put off starting that wedding or birthday gift, or unexpectedly receive an invitation to a baby shower that is only two weeks away. We've provided enough quick pattern stitches to help you start crocheting faster than ever!

Basically, there are two ways to decrease the crochet time required to complete a project:

1. Change a single crochet to a taller stitch: half double crochet, double crochet or even a treble crochet stitch.

2. Use a larger hook.

Additionally, always work in back bar of the chain on row 1 for a more finished look.

Back Bar of Chain

STITCH PATTERN 19 COMPARING LENGTH USING TALLER STITCHES

All four swatches crocheted with a size H hook.

Worked in single crochet

Measures 7½ x 7½ inches

Worked in half double crochet

Measures 7½ x 11½ inches (*length increases 4 inches more than sc—more than 50 percent*)

Worked in double crochet

Measures 7½ x 15 inches *(doubles the length of sc—that's a 100 percent increase!)*

Worked in treble crochet

Measures 7½ x 23½ inches *(increases length 16 inches more than sc, or 300 percent)*

Simply changing to a taller stitch, for example working in treble crochet instead of double crochet, increases the length significantly— fewer rows are required to reach desired length! Because each of the four swatches shown was worked with the same size hook, the width remains constant.

Increasing the height of the stitch means you need to crochet fewer rows with each hook size increase. How easy is that?

Note: Remember to add extra chains to your beginning chain when using taller stitches. You need 1 turning chain for single crochet, 2 chains for half double crochet, 3 chains for double crochet and 4 chains for treble crochet. For example, if the original pattern is a multiple of 6 + 3, that means each pattern repeat takes 6 stitches and the chain-3 is the number of chains to make after turning the end of row. The chain-3 would represent the height of a double crochet and usually counts as the first stitch of the next row, so if you change from double to treble crochet, chain 4 (1 chain increased) instead of chain 3. If the original pattern is worked in single crochet, unless instructed otherwise, chain 1 at the beginning of a new row and follow pattern across. When changing from single crochet to double crochet, you need to add two extra chains to your beginning chain.

ACTUAL CROCHET TIME

While many patterns provide an approximate length of time to make a project, the truth is, everyone works at their own pace. The time required to crochet anything is actual crochet time! It's easy to spend an evening crocheting an afghan and if you begin at 7 p.m. and stop at 10 p.m., you are likely to think you spent three hours crocheting. A phone call from your best friend, fixing a snack, taking a bathroom break or stopping to help a child with homework means those interruptions are not actual crochet time.

There are two quick ways to determine how long it will take you to make any crochet project.

1. A very rough estimate is to figure six to eight hours per skein.

2. After working a few rows of your project, watch the clock and crochet across the next row without interruption—check the clock. If it takes you five minutes to crochet one row, multiply that number (5) times the total number of rows required to determine time required, not including edging or other finishing work. If working on a baby blanket and it takes 20 minutes to crochet across one row and the total number of rows required is 50, 20 (minutes) x 50 (rows) = 1,000 minutes. Divide 1,000 by 60 (minutes in one hour) and the total amount of time required to work the baby blanket is approximately 16½ hours. ■

Stitch Patterns

#1 Little Triangles

PATTERN NOTES

Items shown made with sizes H/8/5mm, I/9/5.5mm, J/10/6mm and K/10½/6.5mm crochet hooks and Bernat Satin medium (worsted) weight yarn.

Pattern is worked in multiples of 4 plus 8 chains.

Chain-3 at beginning of row counts as first double crochet unless otherwise stated.

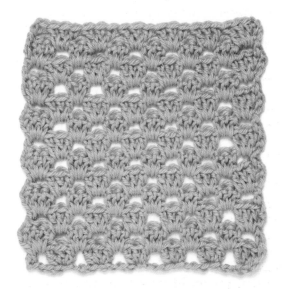

Size J/10/6mm hook = 8 inches square

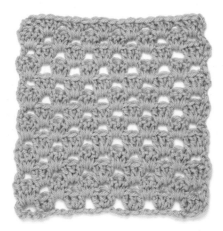

Size H/8/5mm hook = 6½ inches square

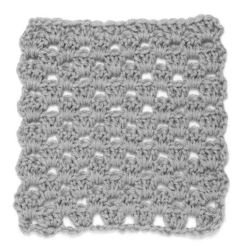

Size I/9/5.5mm hook = 7 inches square

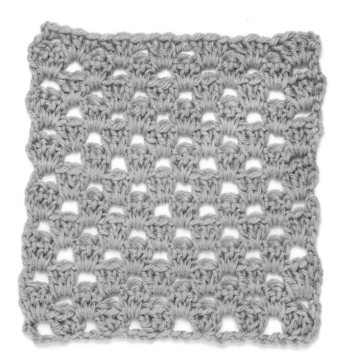

Size K/10½/6.5mm = 9 inches square

INSTRUCTIONS

Row 1: 3 dc in 4th ch from hook (*first 3 chs count as first dc*), sk next 3 chs, [3 dc in next ch, sk next 3 chs] across, ending with dc in last ch, turn.

Row 2: Ch 3 (*see Pattern Notes*), 3 dc in sp between first dc and next dc group, [3 dc in sp between last dc group and next dc group] across, ending with dc in last st, turn.

Rep row 2 for pattern. ■

#2 Triples & V's

PATTERN NOTES

Item shown made with size H/8/5mm crochet hook and Bernat Satin medium (worsted) weight yarn.

Pattern is worked in multiples of 3 plus 6 chains.

Chain-3 at beginning of row counts as first double crochet unless otherwise stated.

SPECIAL STITCH

V-stitch (V-st): (Dc, ch 1, dc) as indicated in instructions.

INSTRUCTIONS

Row 1 (RS): 3 dc in 5th ch from hook (*first 4 chs count as first dc, sk 1 ch*), [sk next 2 chs, 3 dc in next ch] across to last 2 chs, sk next ch, dc in last ch, turn.

Row 2: **Ch 3** (*see Pattern Notes*), **V-st** (*see Special Stitch*) in center dc of each dc group across, ending with dc in last st, turn.

Row 3: Ch 3, 3 dc in ch sp of each V-st across, ending with dc in last st, turn.

Rep rows 2 and 3 alternately for pattern. ■

#3 Pine Trees

PATTERN NOTES

Item shown made with size H/8/5mm crochet
hook and Bernat Satin medium (worsted)
weight yarn.

Yarn is worked in multiples of 10 plus
13 chains.

Chain-3 at beginning of row counts as first
double crochet unless otherwise stated.

Chain-6 at beginning of row counts as
first double crochet and chain-3 unless otherwise stated.

INSTRUCTIONS

Row 1 (RS): Dc in 4th ch from hook (*first 3 chs
count as first dc*), dc in next ch, *ch 2, sk next ch,
dc dec (*see Stitch Guide*) in next 3 chs, ch 2, sk
next ch**, dc in each of next 5 chs, rep from *
across, ending last rep at **, dc in each of last
3 chs, turn.

Row 2: Ch 3 (*see Pattern Notes*), dc dec in next
2 sts, *ch 3, dc in next dc dec, ch 3**, dc dec in
next 2 sts, dc in next dc, dc dec in next 2 sts, rep
from * across, ending last rep at **, dc dec in
next 2 sts, dc in last st, turn.

Row 3: Ch 2, dc in next st (*ch-2 and dc count as
first dec*), *ch 3, 2 dc in next ch-3 sp, dc in next
dc, 2 dc in next ch-3 sp, ch 2**, dc dec in next
3 sts, rep from * across, ending last rep at **, dc
dec in last 2 sts, turn.

Row 4: Ch 6 (*see Pattern Notes*), [dc dec in next 2
sts, dc in next st, dc dec in next 2 sts, ch 3, dc in
next dc dec, ch 3] across, ending with dc in last
st, turn.

Row 5: Ch 3, *2 dc in ch-3 sp, ch 2, sk next st, dc
dec in next 3 sts, 2 dc in next ch sp, dc in next
st**, 2 dc in next st, rep from * across, ending
last rep at **, turn.

Rep rows 2–5 consecutively for pattern. ■

#4 Lickety-Split Lace

PATTERN NOTES
Item shown made with size H/8/5mm crochet hook and Bernat Satin medium (worsted) weight yarn.

Pattern is worked in multiples of 4 plus 2.

Chain-5 at beginning of row counts as first double crochet and chain-2 unless otherwise stated.

Chain-3 at beginning of row counts as first double crochet unless otherwise stated.

INSTRUCTIONS
Row 1 (RS): Sc in 2nd ch from hook, [ch 5, sk next 3 chs, sc in next ch] across, turn.

Row 2: Ch 5 (see Pattern Notes), *sc in next ch sp**, ch 5, rep from * across, ending last rep at **, ch 2, dc in last st, turn.

Row 3: Ch 1, sc in first st, [ch 3, sc in next ch sp] across, turn.

Row 4: Ch 3 (see Pattern Notes), 3 dc in next ch sp, 4 dc in each ch sp across to last ch sp, 3 dc in last ch sp, dc in last st, turn.

Row 5: Ch 1, sc in first st, ch 3, sk next 4 sts, sc in sp between last sk st and next st, [ch 3, sk next 4 sts, sc in next sp between last sk st and next st] across to last 4 sts, ch 3, sk next 3 sts, dc in last st, turn.

Rep rows 2–5 consecutively for pattern. ∎

#5 Endearing

PATTERN NOTES
Item shown made with size H/8/5mm crochet hook and Bernat Satin medium (worsted) weight yarn.

Pattern is worked in multiples of 8 plus 12.

Chain-3 at beginning of row counts as first double crochet unless otherwise stated.

INSTRUCTIONS
Row 1 (RS): Dc in 4th ch from hook (*first 3 chs count as first dc*), *ch 3, sk next 3 chs, sc in next ch, ch 3, sk next 3 chs**, 3 dc in next ch, rep

from * across, ending last rep at **, 2 dc in last ch, turn.

Row 2: Ch 1, sc in first st, *ch 3, **dc dec** *(see Stitch Guide)* in next 2 ch-3 sps, ch 3**, sc in center dc of next dc group, rep from * across, ending last rep at **, 2 dc in last st, turn.

Row 3: **Ch 3** *(see Pattern Notes)*, dc in same st as beg ch-3, *ch 3, sc in next dc dec, ch 3**, 3 dc in next st, rep from * across, ending last rep at **, 2 dc in last st, turn.

Rep rows 2 and 3 alternately for pattern. ∎

#6 Simply Elegant

PATTERN NOTES
Item shown made with size H/8/5mm crochet hook and Bernat Satin medium (worsted) weight yarn.

Pattern is worked in multiples of 10 plus 7 chains.

Chain-3 at beginning of row counts as first double crochet unless otherwise stated.

Chain-5 at beginning of row counts as first double crochet and chain-2 unless otherwise stated.

SPECIAL STITCH
V-stitch (V-st): (Dc, ch 5, dc) as indicated in instructions.

INSTRUCTIONS
Row 1 (RS): Dc in 4th ch from hook *(first 3 chs count as first dc)*, dc in each of next 3 chs, [sk next 2 chs, **V-st** *(see Special Stitch)* in next ch, sk next 2 chs, dc in each of next 5 chs] across, turn.

Row 2: **Ch 3** *(see Pattern Notes)*, dc in each of next 4 sts, [ch 2, sc in ch sp of next V-st, ch 2, sk next dc of V-st, dc in each of next 5 sts] across, turn.

Row 3: Ch 3, sk next st, V-st in next st, [sk next 2 sts, 2 dc in next ch-2 sp, dc in next st, 2 dc in next ch-2 sp, sk next 2 sts, V-st in next st] across to last 2 sts, sk next st, dc in last st, turn.

Row 4: **Ch 5** *(see Pattern Notes)*, sc in ch sp of next V-st, ch 2, [sk next dc of V-st, dc in each of next 5 sts, ch 2, sc in ch sp of next V-st, ch 2] across, dc in last st, turn.

Row 5: Ch 3, dc in next ch-2 sp, dc in next st, [2 dc in next ch-2 sp, sk next 2 sts, V-st in next st, sk next 2 sts, 2 dc in next ch-2 sp, dc in next st] across, dc in last ch-2 sp, dc in last st, turn.

Rep rows 2–5 consecutively for pattern. ∎

#7 Shell Columns

PATTERN NOTES
Item shown made with size H/8/5mm crochet
  hook and Bernat Satin medium (worsted)
  weight yarn.

Pattern is worked in multiples of 11 plus
  8 chains.

Chain-3 at beginning of row counts as first
  double crochet unless otherwise stated.

SPECIAL STITCHES
Shell: (Dc, **picot**—*see Special Stitches,* 4 dc, picot)
  as indicated in instructions.

Picot: Ch 3, sl st in top of last dc worked.

INSTRUCTIONS
Row 1 (RS): Dc in 4th ch from hook (*first 3 chs
  count as first dc*), dc in each of next 4 chs, [sk next
  2 chs, **shell** (*see Special Stitches*) in next ch, sk next
  2 chs, dc in each of next 6 chs] across, turn.

Row 2: Ch 3 (*see Pattern Notes*), dc in each of
  next 5 sts, [ch 2, sk next 2 sts, sc in next st, ch 2,

sk next 2 sts, dc in each of next 6 sts]
across, turn.

Row 3: Ch 3, dc in each of next 5 sts, [shell in
  next st, dc in each of next 6 sts] across, turn.

Rep rows 2 and 3 alternately for pattern. ∎

#8 Awakening

PATTERN NOTES
Item shown made with size H/8/5mm crochet
  hook and Bernat Satin medium (worsted)
  weight yarn.

Pattern is worked in multiples of 14 plus
  4 chains.

Chain-5 at beginning of row counts as
  first double crochet and chain-2 unless
  otherwise stated.

Chain-3 at beginning of row counts as first
  double crochet unless otherwise stated.

SPECIAL STITCHES

V-stitch (V-st): (Dc, ch 1, dc) as indicated in instructions.

Shell: (3 dc, ch 1, 3 dc) as indicated in instructions.

INSTRUCTIONS

Row 1 (RS): Dc in 4th ch from hook (*first 3 chs count as first dc*), dc in each ch across, turn.

Row 2: Ch 5 (*see Pattern Notes*), [sk next 3 sts, **V-st** (*see Special Stitches*) in next st, ch 2, sk next 3 sts, dc in each of next 7 sts, ch 2] across to last st, dc in last st, turn.

Row 3: Ch 3 (*see Pattern Notes*), dc in each of next 7 sts, [**shell** (*see Special Stitches*) in ch-1 sp of next V-st, sk last dc of V-st, dc in each of next 7 sts] across, dc in last st, turn.

Row 4: Ch 5, [V-st in ch-1 sp of next shell, ch 2, sk last 3 dc of shell, dc in each of next 7 sts, ch 2] across, dc in last st, turn.

Row 5: Ch 3, dc in each of next 7 sts, *2 dc in next ch-2 sp, dc in next st, dc in next ch-1 sp, dc in next st, 2 dc in next ch-2 sp**, dc in each of next 7 sts, rep from * across, ending last rep at **, dc in last st, turn.

Row 6: Ch 3, dc in each of next 7 sts, *ch 2, sk next 3 sts, V-st in next st, ch 2, sk next 3 sts**, dc in each of next 7 sts, rep from * across, ending last rep at **, dc in last st, turn.

Row 7: Ch 3, [shell in ch sp of next V-st, dc in each of next 7 sts] across, dc in last st, turn.

Row 8: Ch 3, [dc in each of next 7 sts, ch 2, V-st in ch-1 sp of next shell, ch 2, sk last 3 sts of shell] across, dc in last st, turn.

Row 9: Ch 3, [2 dc in next ch-2 sp, dc in next st, dc in next ch-1 sp, dc in next st, 2 dc in next ch-2 sp, dc in each of next 7 sts] across, dc in last st, turn.

Rep rows 2–9 consecutively for pattern. ∎

#9 Zesty

PATTERN NOTES

Item shown made with size H/8/5mm crochet hook and Bernat Satin medium (worsted) weight yarn.

Pattern is worked in multiples of 7 plus 11 chains.

Chain-3 at beginning of row counts as first double crochet unless otherwise stated.

Chain-4 at beginning of row counts as first double crochet and chain-1 unless otherwise stated.

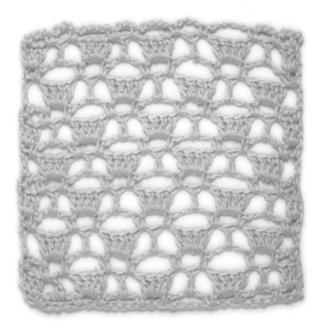

INSTRUCTIONS

Row 1: Sc in 4th ch from hook (*first 3 chs count as first hdc and sk 1 ch*), *ch 4, sk next 4 chs, sc in next ch**, ch 3, sk next ch, sc in next ch, rep from * across, ending last rep at **, ch 1, sk next ch, hdc in last ch, turn.

Row 2 (RS): Ch 3 (*see Pattern Notes*), 2 dc in next ch-1 sp, *ch 1, dc in next ch-4 sp, ch 1**, 4 dc in next ch-3 sp, rep from * across, ending with last rep at **, 2 dc in next ch-1 sp, dc in last st, turn.

Row 3: Ch 1, sc in first st, ch 2, sc in next ch-1 sp, [ch 3, sc in next ch-1 sp, ch 4, sc in next ch-1 sp] across, ending with ch 2, sc in last st, turn.

Row 4: Ch 4 (*see Pattern Notes*), sk next ch sp, [4 dc in next ch-3 sp, ch 1, dc in next ch-4 sp, ch 1] across, ending with sk last ch sp, dc in last st, turn.

Row 5: Ch 3 (*counts as first hdc and ch-1*), *sc in next ch-1 sp, ch 4, sc in next ch-1 sp**, ch 3, rep from * across, ending last rep at **, ch 1, hdc in last st, turn.

Rep rows 2–5 consecutively for pattern. ■

#10 Leaning Shells

PATTERN NOTES
Item shown made with size H/8/5mm crochet hook and Bernat Satin medium (worsted) weight yarn.

Pattern is worked in multiples of 12 plus 7 chains.

Chain-3 at beginning of row counts as first double crochet unless otherwise stated.

SPECIAL STITCH
Shell: 3 dc as indicated in instructions.

INSTRUCTIONS
Row 1 (RS): Dc in 4th ch from hook (*first 3 chs count as first dc*), dc in each of next 3 chs, [ch 3, **shell** (*see Special Stitch*) in next ch, sk next 3 chs, sc in next ch, ch 3, sk next 2 chs, dc in each of next 5 chs] across, turn.

Row 2: Ch 3 (*see Pattern Notes*), dc in each of next 4 sts, [ch 3, shell in next ch-3 sp, sc

in next ch-3 sp, ch 3, dc in each of next 5 sts] across, turn.

Rep row 2 for pattern. ■

#11 Tranquil Trebles

PATTERN NOTES
Item shown made with size H/8/5mm crochet
   hook and Bernat Satin medium (worsted)
   weight yarn.

Pattern is worked in multiples of 4 plus
   8 chains.

Chain-5 at beginning of row counts as
   first treble crochet and chain-1 unless otherwise stated.

Chain-4 counts as first treble crochet unless otherwise stated.

SPECIAL STITCHES
Shell: 4 tr as indicated in instructions.

V-stitch (V-st): (Tr, ch 4, tr) as indicated in
   instructions.

INSTRUCTIONS
Row 1 (RS): Shell *(see Special Stitches)* in 6th ch
   from hook *(first 5 chs count as first tr and sk 1
   ch)*, [sk next 3 chs, shell in next ch] across to
   last 2 chs, sk next ch, tr in last ch, turn.

Row 2: Ch 5 *(see Pattern Notes)*, **tr dec** *(see Stitch
   Guide)* in next 4 tr, [ch 3, tr dec in next 4 sts]
   across, ch 3, tr in last st, turn.

Row 3: Ch 4 *(see Pattern Notes)*, **V-st** *(see Special
   Stitches)* in top of each tr dec across, ending
   with tr in last st, turn.

Row 4: Ch 4, shell in ch sp of each V-st across,
   ending with tr in last st, turn.

Rep rows 2–4 consecutively for pattern. ■

#12 Puffin' Along

PATTERN NOTES

Item shown made with size H/8/5mm crochet hook and Bernat Satin medium (worsted) weight yarn.

Pattern is worked in multiples of 4 plus 7 chains.

Chain-3 at beginning of row counts as first double crochet unless otherwise stated.

SPECIAL STITCHES

V-stitch (V-st): (**Puff st**—*see Special Stitches*, ch 3, puff st) as indicated in instructions.

Puff stitch (puff st): Yo, insert hook as indicated in instructions, yo, pull lp through, [yo, insert hook in same st] twice, yo, pull through all lps on hook.

INSTRUCTIONS

Row 1 (WS): Dc in 4th ch from hook (*first 3 chs count as first dc),* dc in each of next 2 chs, [ch 1, sk next ch, dc in each of next 3 chs] across, ending with dc in last st, turn.

Row 2: **Ch 3** (*see Pattern Notes*), sk next st, **V-st** (*see Special Stitches*) in next st, V-st in center st of each dc group across, ending with dc in last st, turn.

Row 3: Ch 3, 3 dc in ch sp of next V-st, [ch 1, 3 dc in ch sp of next V-st across, ending with dc in last st, turn.

Rep rows 2 and 3 alternately for pattern. ∎

#13 Puffection

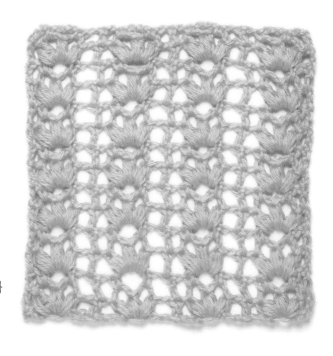

PATTERN NOTES

Item shown made with size H/8/5mm crochet hook and Bernat Satin medium (worsted) weight yarn.

Pattern is worked in multiples of 8 plus 12 chains.

Chain-4 at beginning of row counts as first double crochet and chain-1 unless otherwise stated.

SPECIAL STITCHES

Shell: (**Puff st**—*see Special Stitches*, {ch 3, puff st} twice) as indicated in instructions.

Puff stitch (puff st): Yo, insert hook as indicated in instructions, yo, pull lp through, [yo, insert hook in same st] twice, yo, pull through all lps on hook.

INSTRUCTIONS

Row 1 (RS): **Shell** (*see Special Stitches*) in 7th ch from hook (*first 7 chs count as first dc and sk 3 chs*), *sk next 3 chs, dc in next ch**, sk next 3 chs, shell in next ch, rep from * across, ending last rep at **, turn.

Row 2: **Ch 4** (*see Pattern Notes*), *sc in next ch-3 sp, ch 3, sc in next ch-3 sp, ch 1, dc in next dc**, ch 1, rep from * across, ending last rep at **, turn.

Row 3: Ch 4, *shell in next ch-3 sp, ch 1, dc in next dc**, ch 1, rep from * across, ending last rep at **, turn.

Rep rows 2 and 3 alternately for pattern. ■

#14 Tryst

PATTERN NOTES

Item shown made with size H/8/5mm crochet hook and Bernat Satin medium (worsted) weight yarn.

Pattern is worked in multiples of 8 plus 11 chains.

Chain-4 at beginning of row counts as first double crochet and chain-1 unless otherwise stated.

SPECIAL STITCHES

V-stitch (V-st): (Dc, ch 2, dc) as indicated in instructions.

Shell: (Cl—*see Special Stitches*, ch 2, cl) as indicated in instructions.

Cluster (cl): Holding back last lp of each st on hook, 3 dc as indicated in instructions, yo, pull through all lps on hook.

INSTRUCTIONS

Row 1 (RS): Dc in 5th ch from hook (*first 4 chs count as first dc and ch-1*), ch 2, sc in next ch, ch 3, sk next ch, sc in next ch, [ch 2, sk next 2 chs, **V-st** (*see Special Stitches*) in next ch, ch 2, sk next 2 chs, sc in next ch, ch 3, sk next ch, sc in last ch] across to last 3 chs, sk next 2 chs, (dc, ch 1, dc) in last st, turn.

Row 2: Ch 1, sc in first st, *ch 2, **shell** (*see Special Stitches*) in next ch-3 sp, ch 2**, sc in ch sp of next V-st, rep from * across, ending last rep at **, sc in last st, turn.

Row 3: Ch 1, sc in first st, ch 1, sc in next ch-2 sp, *ch 2, V-st in ch-2 sp of next shell, ch 2, sc in next ch-2 sp**, ch 3, sc in next ch-2 sp, rep from * across, ending last rep at **, ch 1, sc in last st, turn.

Row 4: **Ch 4** (*see Pattern Notes*), cl in next ch-1 sp, *ch 2, sc in ch sp of next V-st, ch 2**, shell in next ch-2 sp, rep from * across, ending last rep at **, cl in last ch-1 sp, ch 1, dc in last st, turn.

Row 5: Ch 4, dc in same st as beg ch-4, *ch 2, sc in next ch-2 sp, ch 3, sc in next ch-2 sp**, ch 2, V-st in ch sp of next shell, rep from * across, ending last rep at **, ch 2, (dc, ch 1, dc) in last st, turn.

Rep rows 2–5 consecutively for pattern. ■

#15 Duet

PATTERN NOTES
Item shown made with size H/8/5mm crochet
hook and Bernat Satin medium (worsted)
weight yarn.

Pattern is worked in multiples of 8 plus 12 chains.

Chain-3 at beginning of row counts as first
double crochet unless otherwise stated.

SPECIAL STITCHES
Shell: (**Cl**—*see Special Stitches*, ch 2, cl) as
indicated in instructions.

Cluster (cl): Holding back last lp of each st on
hook, 3 dc as indicated in instructions, yo, pull
through all lps on hook.

V-stitch (V-st): (Dc, ch 2, dc) as indicated in
instructions.

INSTRUCTIONS
Row 1 (RS): Dc in 4th ch from hook (*first 3 chs
count as first dc*), sk next 3 chs, *shell (*see Special
Stitches*) in next ch, sk next 3 chs**, **V-st** (*see
Special Stitches*) in next ch, sk next 3 chs, rep
from * across, ending last rep at **, ending with
2 dc in last st, turn.

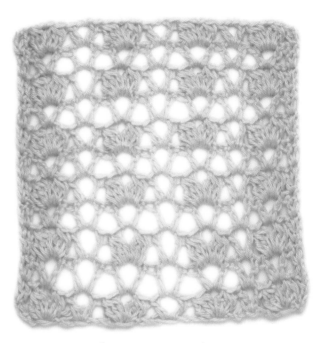

Row 2: **Ch 3** (*see Pattern Notes*), dc in same st
as beg ch-3, V-st in ch sp of each shell and each
V-st across, 2 dc in last st, turn.

Row 3: Ch 3, dc in same st as beg ch-3, *shell in
ch sp of next V-st**, V-st in ch sp of next V-st,
rep from * across, ending last rep at **, 2 dc in
last st, turn.

Rep rows 2 and 3 alternately for pattern. ∎

#16 Scrunch

PATTERN NOTES
Item shown made with size H/8/5mm crochet
hook and Bernat Satin medium (worsted)
weight yarn.

Pattern is worked in multiples of 3 plus 8 chains.

Chain-4 at beginning of row counts as
first double crochet and chain-1 unless
otherwise stated.

SPECIAL STITCHES
V-stitch (V-st): (Dc, ch 1, dc) as indicated in
instructions.

Puff stitch (puff st): Yo, insert hook as indicated in instructions, yo, pull lp through, yo, insert hook in same place, yo, pull lp through, yo, pull through all lps on hook.

INSTRUCTIONS

Row 1 (RS): **V-st** (*see Special Stitches*) in 6th ch from hook (*first 5 chs count as first dc and sk 2 chs*), [sk next 2 chs, V-st in next ch] across to last 2 chs, sk next ch, dc in last ch, turn.

Row 2: Ch 1, sc in first st, *ch 3, **puff st** (*see Special Stitches*) in ch sp of next V-st, ch 3**, sc in sp between V-sts, rep from * across, ending last rep at **, sc in last st, turn.

Row 3: **Ch 4** (*see Pattern Notes*), V-st in each puff st across, dc in last st, turn.

Rep rows 2 and 3 alternately for pattern. ∎

#17 Lace Bands

PATTERN NOTES

Item shown made with size H/8/5mm crochet hook and Bernat Satin medium (worsted) weight yarn.

Pattern is worked in multiples of 8 plus 3 chains.

Chain-3 at beginning of row counts as first double crochet unless otherwise stated.

SPECIAL STITCH

Cluster (cl): Holding back last lp of each st on hook, 3 dc as indicated in instructions, yo, pull through all lps on hook.

INSTRUCTIONS

Row 1 (RS): Dc in 4th ch from hook (*first 3 chs count as first dc*), dc in each ch across, turn.

Row 2: Ch 1, sc in first st, [ch 3, sk next 3 sts, (**cl**—*see Special Stitch*, ch 3, cl) in next st, ch 3, sk next 3 sts, sc in next st] across, turn.

Row 3: Ch 2, dc in next ch-3 sp (*ch-2 and dc count as first dc dec*), *ch 3, (sc, {ch 3, sc} twice) in ch-3 sp between cl, ch 3**, **dc dec** (*see Stitch Guide*) in next 2 ch-3 sps, rep from * across, ending last rep at **, dc dec in last ch-3 sp and last st, turn.

Row 4: **Ch 3** (*see Pattern Notes*), 2 dc in same st as beg ch-3, ch 3, [5 dc in next dc dec, ch 3] across, ending with 3 dc in last st, turn.

Row 5: Ch 3, dc in each st and in each ch across, turn.

Rep rows 2–5 consecutively for pattern. ∎

#18 Game Board

DOUBLE CROCHET VERSION

PATTERN NOTES

Item shown made with size H/8/5mm crochet hook and Bernat Satin medium (worsted) weight yarn.

Pattern is worked in multiples of 10 plus 9 chains.

Chain-3 at beginning of row counts as first double crochet unless otherwise stated.

Chain-5 at beginning of row counts as first double crochet and chain-2 unless otherwise stated.

SPECIAL STITCHES

Decrease (dec): Holding back last lp of each st on hook, dc in next st or ch, sk next 3 sts or chs, dc in next st or ch, yo, pull through all lps on hook.

Popcorn (pc): 5 dc as indicated in instructions, drop lp from hook, insert hook in first dc of dc group, pull dropped lp through. Push pc to WS of work.

INSTRUCTIONS

Row 1 (RS): Dc in 4th ch from hook (*first 3 chs count as first dc*), dc in each of next 4 chs, [ch 3, **dec** (*see Special Stitches*), ch 3, dc in each of next 5 chs] across, ending with dc in last ch, turn.

Row 2: Ch 3 (*see Pattern Notes*), dc in each of next 5 sts, [ch 2, **pc** (*see Special Stitch*) in next dec, ch 2, dc in each of next 5 sts] across, dc in last st, turn.

Row 3: Ch 5 (*see Pattern Notes*), dec in next dc group, ch 2, *2 dc in next ch-2 sp, dc in next pc, 2 dc in next ch-2 sp, ch 2, dec in next dc group, ch 2, rep from * across, dc in last st, turn.

Row 4: Ch 5, pc in next dc dec, ch 2, [dc in each of next 5 sts, ch 2, pc in next dc dec, ch 2] across, ending with dc in last st, turn.

Row 5: Ch 3, *2 dc in next ch-2 sp, dc in next pc, 2 dc in next ch-2 sp**, ch 2, dec in next dc

group, ch 2, rep from * across, ending last rep at **, dc in last st, turn.

Rep rows 2–5 consecutively for pattern.

TREBLE CROCHET VERSION

PATTERN NOTES

Item shown made with size H/8/5mm crochet hook and Bernat Satin medium (worsted) weight yarn.

Pattern is worked in multiples of 10 plus 10 chains.

Chain-4 at beginning of row counts as first treble crochet unless otherwise stated.

Chain-6 at beginning of row counts as first treble crochet and chain-2 unless otherwise stated.

SPECIAL STITCHES

Decrease (dec): Holding back last lp of each st on hook, tr in next st or ch, sk next 3 sts or chs, tr in next st or ch, yo, pull through all lps on hook.

Popcorn (pc): 5 tr as indicated in instructions, drop lp from hook, insert hook in first dc of dc group, pull dropped lp through. Push pc to WS of work.

INSTRUCTIONS

Row 1 (RS): Tr in 5th ch from hook (*first 4 chs count as first tr*), tr in each of next 4 chs, [ch 3, **dec** (*see Stitch Guide*), tr in each of next 5 chs] across, ending with tr in last ch, turn.

Row 2: **Ch 4** (*see Pattern Notes*), tr in each of next 5 sts, [ch 2, **pc** (*see Special Stitch*) in next dec, ch 2, tr in each of next 5 sts] across, tr in last st, turn.

Row 3: **Ch 6** (*see Pattern Notes*), dec in next tr group, ch 2, *2 tr in next ch-2 sp, tr in next pc, 2 tr in next ch-2 sp, ch 2, dec in next tr group, ch 2, rep from * across, tr in last st, turn.

Row 4: Ch 6, pc in next tr dec, ch 2, [tr in each of next 5 sts, ch 2, pc in next tr dec, ch 2] across, ending with tr in last st, turn.

Row 5: Ch 4, *2 tr in next ch-2 sp, tr in next pc, 2 tr in next ch-2 sp**, ch 2, dec in first next tr group, ch 2, rep from * across, ending last rep at **, tr in last st, turn.

Rep rows 2–5 consecutively for pattern. ■

#19 Bobbled Arches

PATTERN NOTES

Items shown made with size H/8/5mm crochet hook and Bernat Satin medium (worsted) weight yarn.

Single crochet pattern is worked in multiples of 6 plus 10 chains.

Half double crochet pattern is worked in multiples of 6 plus 10 chains.

Double crochet pattern is worked in multiples of 6 plus 11 chains.

Treble crochet pattern is worked in multiples of 6 plus 12 chains.

Chain-2 at beginning of row counts as first half double crochet unless otherwise stated.

Chain-3 at beginning of row counts as first double crochet unless otherwise stated.

Chain-4 at beginning of row counts as first treble crochet unless otherwise stated.

SPECIAL STITCHES

Single crochet popcorn (sc pc): 5 sc as indicated in instructions, drop lp from hook, insert hook in first sc of sc group, pull dropped lp through.

Half double crochet popcorn (hdc pc): 5 hdc as indicated in instructions, drop lp from hook, insert hook in first hdc of hdc group, pull dropped lp through.

Double crochet popcorn (dc pc): 5 dc as indicated in instructions, drop lp from hook, insert hook in first dc of dc group, pull dropped lp through.

Treble crochet popcorn (tr pc): 5 tr as indicated in instructions, drop lp from hook, insert hook in first tr of tr group, pull dropped lp through.

INSTRUCTIONS

SINGLE CROCHET VERSION

Row 1 (RS): Sc in 2nd ch from hook and in each ch across, turn.

Rows 2–4: Ch 1, sc in each st across, turn.

Row 5: Ch 1, sc in first st, **sc pc** *(see Special Stitches)* in next st, [ch 3, sk next 2 sts, sc in next st, ch 3, sk next 2 sts, sc pc in next st] across, ending with sc in last st, turn.

Row 6: Ch 1, sc in first st, sc in next sc pc, *sc in next ch sp, ch 3, sc in next ch sp, sc in next sc pc**, sc in next ch sp, ch 3, rep from * across, ending last rep at **, sc in last st, turn.

Row 7: Ch 1, sc in each st across with 3 sc in each ch-3 sp, turn.

Rep rows 2–7 consecutively for pattern.

HALF DOUBLE CROCHET VERSION

Row 1 (RS): Hdc in 2nd ch from hook and in each ch across, turn.

Rows 2–4: **Ch 2** *(see Pattern Notes)*, hdc in each st across, turn.

Row 5: Ch 2, **hdc pc** *(see Special Stitches)* in next st, [ch 3, sk next 2 sts, hdc in next st, ch 3, sk next 2 sts, hdc pc in next st] across, ending with sc in last st, turn.

Row 6: Ch 2, hdc in next pc, *hdc in next ch sp, ch 3, hdc in next ch sp, hdc in next hdc pc**, hdc in next ch sp, ch 3, rep from * across, ending last rep at **, hdc in last st, turn.

Row 7: Ch 2, hdc in each st across with 3 hdc in each ch-3 sp, turn.

Rep rows 2–7 consecutively for pattern.

DOUBLE CROCHET VERSION

Row 1 (RS): Dc in 4th ch from hook (*first 3 chs count as first dc*) and in each ch across, turn.

Rows 2–4: **Ch 3** (*see Pattern Notes*), dc in each st across, turn.

Row 5: Ch 3, **dc pc** (*see Special Stitches*) in next st, [ch 3, sk next 2 sts, dc in next st, ch 3, sk next 2 sts, dc pc in next st] across, ending with sc in last st, turn.

Row 6: Ch 3, dc in next dc pc, *dc in next ch sp, ch 3, dc in next ch sp, dc in next dc pc**, dc in next ch sp, ch 3, rep from * across, ending last rep at **, dc in last st, turn.

Row 7: Ch 3, dc in each st across with 3 dc in each ch-3 sp, turn.

Rep rows 2–7 consecutively for pattern.

TREBLE CROCHET VERSION

Row 1 (RS): Tr in 5th ch from hook (*first 4 chs count as first tr*) and in each ch across, turn.

Rows 2–4: **Ch 4** (*see Pattern Notes*), tr in each st across, turn.

Row 5: Ch 4, **tr pc** (*see Special Stitches*) in next st, [ch 3, sk next 2 sts, tr in next st, ch 3, sk next 2 sts, tr pc in next st] across, ending with sc in last st, turn.

Row 6: Ch 4, tr in next tr pc, *tr in next ch sp, ch 3, tr in next ch sp, tr in next tr pc**, tr in next ch sp, ch 3, rep from * across, ending last rep at **, tr in last st, turn.

Row 7: Ch 4, tr in each st across with 3 tr in each ch-3 sp, turn.

Rep rows 2–7 consecutively for pattern. ■

#20 Quick Wrap

PATTERN NOTES

Item shown made with size H/8/5mm crochet hook and Bernat Satin medium (worsted) weight yarn.

Pattern is worked in multiples of 2 plus 5 chains.

Chain-4 at beginning of row counts as first double crochet and chain-1 unless otherwise stated.

Chain-3 at beginning of row counts as first double crochet unless otherwise stated.

SPECIAL STITCH

Wrap: [Yo, insert hook around post of last dc worked, pull up lp] 3 times, yo, pull through all lps on hook.

INSTRUCTIONS

Row 1 (RS): Dc in 4th ch from hook (*first 3 chs count as first dc*), dc in each ch across, turn.

Row 2: Ch 4 (*see Pattern Notes*), sk next st, dc in next st, [ch 1, sk next st, dc in next st] across, turn.

Row 3: Ch 3 (*see Pattern Notes*), *(dc, **wrap**— *see Special Stitch*, ch 1) in next st, ch 1, dc in next st**, ch 1, rep from * across, ending last rep at **, turn.

Row 4: Ch 4, *dc in next wrap, ch 1, dc in next st**, ch 1, rep from * across, ending last rep at **, turn.

Row 5: Ch 3, dc in each ch sp and in each st across, turn.

Rep rows 2–5 consecutively for pattern. ∎

#21 Rising Sun

PATTERN NOTES

Item shown made with size H/8/5mm crochet hook and Bernat Satin medium (worsted) weight yarn.

Pattern is worked in multiples of 24 plus 6 chains.

Chain-6 at beginning of row counts as first double crochet and chain-3 unless otherwise stated.

Chain-4 at beginning of row counts as first double crochet and chain-1 unless otherwise stated.

Chain-7 at beginning of row counts as first double crochet and chain-4 unless otherwise stated.

Chain-3 at beginning of row counts as first double crochet unless otherwise stated.

SPECIAL STITCHES

V-stitch (V-st): (Dc, ch 1, dc) as indicated in instructions.

Puff stitch (puff st): [Yo, insert hook as indicated in instructions, yo, pull lp through] 3 times, yo, pull through all lps on hook.

INSTRUCTIONS

Row 1 (RS): V-st (*see Special Stitches*) in 4th ch from hook (*first 4 chs count as first dc and sk 1 ch*), [sk next 2 chs, V-st in next ch] across to last 2 chs, sk next ch, dc in last st, turn.

Row 2: Ch 6 (*see Pattern Notes*), sk next V-st, V-st in ch sp of next V-st, ch 3, sk next V-st, [V-st in ch sp of each of next 3 V-sts, ch 3, sk next V-st, V-st in ch sp of next V-st, ch 3] across, ending with dc in last st, turn.

Row 3: Ch 4 (*see Pattern Notes*), *puff st (*see Special Stitches*) in first dc of next V-st, ch 2, dc in ch sp of same V-st, puff st in last dc of same V-st**, ch 2, V-st in ch sp of each of next 3 V-sts, ch 2, rep from * across, ending last rep at **, ch 1, dc in last st, turn.

Row 4: Ch 6, sc in next ch-2 sp, ch 3, sc in next ch-2 sp, ch 3, [V-st in ch sp of each of next 3 V-sts, ch 3, sc in next ch-2 sp, ch 3, sc in next ch-2 sp, ch 3] across, ending with dc in last st, turn.

Row 5: Ch 4, sk next ch-3 sp, *(puff st, {ch 3, puff st} 3 times) in next ch-3 sp**, ch 2, V-st in ch sp of each of next 3 V-sts, ch 2, rep from * across, ending last rep at **, ch 1, sk last ch-3 sp, dc in last st, turn.

Row 6: Ch 7 (*see Pattern Notes*), sk next 2 ch sps, sc in next ch-3 sp, ch 4, [V-st in ch sp of each of next 3 V-sts, ch 4, sk next 2 ch sps, sc in next ch sp, ch 4] across, dc in last st, turn.

Row 7: Ch 3 (*see Pattern Notes*), *V-st in next ch sp, V-st in next st, V-st in next ch sp**, V-st in ch sp of each of next 3 V-sts, rep from * across, ending last rep at **, dc in last st, turn.

Row 8: Ch 3, *V-st in ch sp of each of next 3 V-sts**, ch 3, sk next V-st, V-st in ch sp of next V-st, ch 3, sk next V-st, rep from * across, ending last rep at **, dc in last st, turn.

Row 9: Ch 3, *V-st in ch sp of each of next 3 V-sts**, ch 2, puff st in first st of next V-st, ch 2, dc in ch sp of same V-st, ch 2, puff st in last st of same V-st, ch 2, rep from * across, ending last rep at **, dc in last st, turn.

Row 10: Ch 3, *V-st in ch sp of each of next 3 V-sts**, ch 3, sk next ch-2 sp, sc in next ch-2 sp, ch 3, sc in next ch-2 sp, ch 3, rep from * across, ending last rep at **, dc in last st, turn.

Row 11: Ch 3, *V-st in ch sp of each of next 3 V-sts**, ch 2, sk next ch sp, (puff st, {ch 3, puff st} 3 times) in next ch-3 sp, ch 2, rep from * across, ending last rep at **, turn.

Row 12: Ch 3, *V-st in ch sp of each of next 3 V-sts**, ch 4, sk next 2 ch sps, sc in next ch sp, ch 4, sk next 2 ch sps, rep from * across, ending last rep at **, dc in last st, turn.

Row 13: Ch 3, *V-st in ch sp of each of next 3 V-sts**, V-st in next ch sp, V-st in next st, V-st in next ch sp, rep from * across, ending last rep at **, dc in last st, turn.

Rep rows 2–13 consecutively for pattern. ∎

#22 Spaced Diamonds

PATTERN NOTES

Item shown made with size H/8/5mm crochet
   hook and Bernat Satin medium (worsted)
   weight yarn.

Pattern is worked in multiples of 10 plus 17 chains.

Chain-3 at beginning of row counts as first
   double crochet unless otherwise stated.

Chain-4 at beginning of row counts as
   first double crochet and chain-1 unless
   otherwise stated.

INSTRUCTIONS

Row 1 (RS): Dc in 6th ch from hook (*first 5 chs
count as first dc, sk 1 ch and ch-1*), dc in each of
next 9 chs, [ch 2, sk next 2 chs, dc in each of
next 10 chs] across to last 2 chs, sk next ch, dc
in last ch, turn.

Row 2: Ch 3 (*see Pattern Notes*), dc in next ch-1 sp,
ch 2, sk next 2 sts, dc in each of next 6 sts, ch 2, sk
next 2 sts, [2 dc in next ch sp, ch 2, sk next 2 sts,
dc in each of next 6 sts, ch 2, sk next 2 sts] across,
ending with dc in last ch sp, dc in last st, turn.

Row 3: Ch 3, dc in next st, 2 dc in next ch sp, *ch 2,
sk next 2 sts, dc in each of next 2 dc, ch 2, sk next
2 dc, 2 dc in next ch sp**, dc in each of next 2 sts,
2 dc in next ch sp, rep from * across, ending last
rep at **, dc in each of last 2 sts, turn.

Row 4: Ch 3, dc in each of next 3 sts, 2 dc in next
ch sp, ch 2, sk next 2 sts, [dc in next ch sp, dc
in each of next 6 sts, 2 dc in next ch sp, ch 2, sk
next 2 sts] across to last ch sp, 2 dc in last ch sp,
dc in each of last 4 sts, turn.

Row 5: Ch 3, dc in each of next 3 sts, *ch 2,
sk next 2 sts, 2 dc in next ch sp, ch 2, sk next
2 sts**, dc in each of next 6 sts, rep from *
across, ending last rep at **, dc in each of last
4 sts, turn.

Row 6: Ch 3, dc in next st, *ch 2, sk next 2 sts,
2 dc in next ch sp, ch 2, sk next 2 sts**, dc in
each of next 6 sts, rep from * across, ending last
rep at **, dc in each of last 2 sts, turn.

Row 7: Ch 4 (*see Pattern Notes*), sk next st, *2
dc in next ch sp, dc in each of next 6 sts, 2 dc
in next ch sp**, ch 2, sk next 2 sts, rep from *
across, ending last rep at **, ch 1, sk next st,
dc in last st, turn.

Rep rows 2–7 consecutively for pattern. ■

#23 Combo

PATTERN NOTES

Item shown made with size H/8/5mm crochet hook and Bernat Satin medium (worsted) weight yarn.

Pattern is worked in multiples of 8 plus 7 chains.

Chain-3 at beginning of row counts as first double crochet unless otherwise stated.

Chain-5 at beginning of row counts as first double crochet and chain-2 unless otherwise stated.

Chain-4 at beginning of row counts as first double crochet and chain-1 unless otherwise stated.

SPECIAL STITCH

Shell: 5 dc as indicated in instructions.

INSTRUCTIONS

Row 1 (RS): Dc in 4th ch from hook (*first 3 chs count as first dc*), and in each ch across, turn.

Row 2: Ch 3 (*see Pattern Notes*), dc in each st across, turn.

Row 3: Ch 1, sc in first st, [ch 5, sk next 3 sts, sc in next st] across, turn.

Row 4: Ch 5 (*see Pattern Notes*), *sc in next ch-5 sp**, ch 5, rep from * across, ending last rep at **, ch 2, dc in last st, turn.

Row 5: Ch 1, sc in first st, *shell (*see Special Stitch*) in next sc**, sc in next ch-5 sp, sc in last st, turn.

Row 6: Ch 4 (*see Pattern Notes*), *sc in center dc of next shell**, ch 3, sc in next ch-5 sp, rep from * across, ending last rep at **, ch 1, dc in last st, turn.

Row 7: Ch 3, dc in next ch-1 sp, [3 dc in next sc, 3 dc in next ch-3 sp] across, ending with dc in last ch-1 sp, dc in last st, turn.

Rep rows 2–7 consecutively for pattern. ∎

#24 Standout

PATTERN NOTES

Item shown made with size H/8/5mm crochet hook and Bernat Satin medium (worsted) weight yarn.

Pattern is worked in multiples of 14 plus 11 chains.

Chain-3 at beginning of row counts as first double crochet unless otherwise stated.

SPECIAL STITCH

Shell: Dc as indicated in instructions, ch 3, 3 dc around post of dc just worked.

INSTRUCTIONS

Row 1 (RS): Dc in 4th ch from hook (*first 3 chs count as first dc*), sk next 2 chs, **shell** (*see Special Stitch*) in next ch, sk next 2 chs, [dc in next ch, ch 2, sk next 3 chs, 3 dc in next ch, ch 2, sk next 3 chs, dc in next ch, sk next 2 chs, shell in next ch, sk next 2 chs] across, ending with dc in each of last 2 chs, turn.

Row 2: Ch 3 (*see Pattern Notes*), **bpdc** (*see Stitch Guide*) around next st, *ch 2, sc in next ch-3 sp of shell, ch 2, bpdc around next st**, ch 1, 2 dc in next st, dc in next st, 2 dc in next st, ch 1, bpdc around next st, rep from * across, ending last rep at **, dc in last st, turn.

Row 3: Ch 3, **fpdc** (*see Stitch Guide*) around next bpdc, *shell in next sc, fpdc around next bpdc**, 2 dc in next st, dc in each of next 3 sts, 2 dc in next st, fpdc around next bpdc, rep from * around, ending last rep at **, dc in last st, turn.

Row 4: Ch 3, bpdc around next fpdc, *ch 2, sc in ch sp of next shell, ch 2, bpdc around next fpdc**, ch 2, sk next 3 sts, 3 dc in next st, ch 2, fpdc around next fpdc, rep from * across, ending last rep at **, dc in last st, turn.

Row 5: Ch 3, fpdc around next bpdc, *shell in next sc, fpdc around next bpdc**, ch 1, 2 dc in next st, dc in next st, 2 dc in next st, ch 2, fpdc around next bpdc, rep from * across, ending last rep at **, dc in last st, turn.

Row 6: Ch 3, bpdc around next fpdc, *ch 2, sc in ch sp of next shell, ch 2, bpdc around next fpdc**, 2 dc in next st, dc in each of next 3 sts, 2 dc in next st, bpdc around next fpdc, rep from * across, ending last rep at **, dc in last st, turn.

Row 7: Ch 3, fpdc around next bpdc, *shell in next sc, fpdc around next bpdc**, ch 2, sk next 3 sts, 3 dc in next st, ch 2, fpdc around next bpdc, rep from * across, ending last rep at **, dc in last st, turn.

Rep rows 2–7 consecutively for pattern. ■

#25 Calypso

PATTERN NOTES

Item shown made with size H/8/5mm crochet
hook and Bernat Satin medium (worsted)
weight yarn.

Pattern is worked in multiples of 8 plus
2 chains.

Chain-3 at beginning of row counts as first
double crochet unless otherwise stated.

Chain-4 at beginning of row counts as
first double crochet and chain-1 unless
otherwise stated.

SPECIAL STITCHES

Shell: (3 dc, ch 3, 3 dc) as indicated in
instructions.

V-stitch (V-st): (Dc, ch 1, dc) as indicated in
instructions.

INSTRUCTIONS

Row 1 (RS): Sc in 2nd ch from hook, [ch 1, sk
next 3 chs, **shell** (see Special Stitches) in next ch,
ch 1, sk next 3 chs, sc in next ch] across, turn.

Row 2: **Ch 3** (see Pattern Notes), dc in same st
as beg ch-3, *ch 2, (sc, ch 3, sc) in ch sp of next
shell, ch 2**, **V-st** (see Special Stitches) in next
sc, rep from * across, ending last rep at **, 2 dc
in last st, turn.

Row 3: **Ch 4** (see Pattern Notes), 3 dc in same
st as beg ch-4, *ch 1, sc in next ch-3 sp, ch 1**,
shell in ch sp of next V-st, rep from * across,
ending last rep at **, (3 dc, ch 1, dc) in last st,
turn.

Row 4: Ch 1, sc in first st, sc in next ch-1 sp, *ch 2,
V-st in next sc, ch 2**, (sc, ch 3, sc) in next ch-3
sp, rep from * across, ending last rep at **, sc in
last ch-1 sp, sc in last st, turn.

Row 5: Ch 1, sc in first st, *ch 1, shell in ch sp of
next V-st, ch 1**, sc in next ch-3 sp, rep from *
across, ending last rep at **, sc in last st, turn.

Rep rows 2–5 consecutively for pattern. ■

#26 Picot Shells

PATTERN NOTES
Item shown made with size H/8/5mm crochet hook and Bernat Satin medium (worsted) weight yarn.

Pattern is worked in multiples of 8 plus 12 chains.

Chain-3 at beginning of row counts as first double crochet unless otherwise stated.

SPECIAL STITCHES
Picot: Ch 3, sl st in top of last dc worked.

Shell: (3 dc, ch 3, 3 dc) as indicated in instructions.

INSTRUCTIONS
Row 1 (RS): 3 dc in 4th ch from hook (*first 3 chs count as first dc*), **picot** (*see Special Stitches*), *sk next 7 chs**, **shell** (*see Special Stitches*) in next ch, picot, rep from * across, ending last rep at **, 4 dc in last st, turn.

Row 2: **Ch 3** (*see Pattern Notes*), 3 dc in same st as beg ch-3, picot, [shell in ch sp of next shell, picot] across, ending with 4 dc in last st, turn.

Rep row 2 for pattern. ∎

#27 Treble Rhapsody

PATTERN NOTES
Item shown made with size H/8/5mm crochet hook and Bernat Satin medium (worsted) weight yarn.

Pattern is worked in multiples of 12 plus 16 chains.

Chain-4 at beginning of row counts as first treble crochet unless otherwise stated.

Chain-9 at beginning of row counts as first treble crochet and chain-5 unless otherwise stated.

SPECIAL STITCHES
Puff stitch (puff st): [Yo, insert hook as indicated in instructions, yo, pull lp through st] twice, yo, pull through all lps on hook.

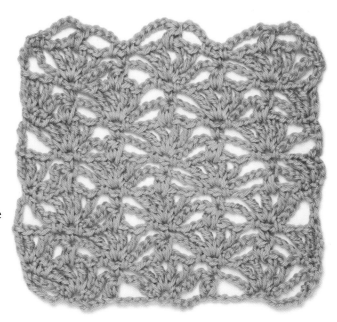

Shell: (Tr, {ch 1, tr} 3 times) as indicated in instructions.

INSTRUCTIONS

Row 1 (WS): Sc in 9th ch from hook (*first 8 chs count as first tr and sk 4 chs*), ch 1, sk next ch, sc in next ch, ch 4, sk next 4 chs, [**puff st** (*see Special Stitches*) in next ch, ch 4, sk next 4 chs, sc in next ch, ch 1, sk next ch, sc in next ch, ch 4, sk next 4 chs] across, tr in last ch, turn.

Row 2: Ch 1, sc in first st, ch 2, *shell (*see Special Stitches*) in next ch-1 sp, ch 2**, sc in next puff st, ch 2, rep from * across, ending last rep at **, sc in last st, turn.

Row 3: Ch 1, sc in first st, sc in next ch-2 sp, ch 4, sk next st, next ch-1 sp and next st, puff st in next ch-1 sp, ch 4, sk next st, next ch-1 sp and

next st, sc in next ch-2 sp**, ch 1, sc in next ch-2 sp, rep from * across, ending last rep at **, sc in last st, turn.

Row 4: Ch 4 (*see Pattern Notes*), (tr, ch 1, tr) in same st as beg ch-4, ch 2, sc in next puff st, ch 2, *shell in next ch-1 sp, ch 2**, sc in next puff st, ch 2, rep from * across, ending last rep at **, (tr, ch 1, 2 tr) in last st, turn.

Row 5: Ch 9 (*see Pattern Notes*), *sc in next ch-2 sp, ch 1, sc in next ch-2 sp, ch 5**, puff st in center ch sp of next shell, ch 5, rep from * across, ending last rep at **, tr in last st, turn.

Rep rows 2–5 consecutively for pattern. ■

#28 Simplicity

PATTERN NOTES

Item shown made with size H/8/5mm crochet hook and Bernat Satin medium (worsted) weight yarn.

Pattern is worked in multiples of 12 plus 7 chains.

Chain-3 at beginning of row counts as first double crochet unless otherwise stated.

SPECIAL STITCH

Shell: (2 dc, ch 1, 2 dc) as indicated in instructions.

INSTRUCTIONS

Row 1 (RS): Dc in 4th ch from hook (*first 3 chs count as first dc*), dc in each of next 3 chs, [ch 1, sk next 3 chs, **shell** (*see Special Stitch*) in next ch, ch 1, sk next 3 chs, dc in each of next 5 chs] across, turn.

Row 2: Ch 3 (*see Pattern Notes*), dc in each of next 4 sts, [ch 1, shell in ch sp of next shell,

ch 1, sk next 2 sts of shell, dc in each of next 5 sts] across, turn.

Rep row 2 for pattern. ■

#29 Concurrence

PATTERN NOTES
Item shown made with size H/8/5mm crochet hook and Bernat Satin medium (worsted) weight yarn.

Pattern is worked in multiples of 8 plus 2 chains.

SPECIAL STITCH
Shell: (3 dc, ch 5, 3 dc) as indicated in instructions.

INSTRUCTIONS
Row 1 (RS): Sc in 2nd ch from hook, [sk next 3 chs, **shell** *(see Special Stitch)* in next ch, sk next 3 chs, sc in next ch] across, turn.

Row 2: Ch 3, sk next 2 sts, dc in next st *(first ch-3 and dc count as dc dec)*, *ch 3, sc in ch sp of next shell, ch 3**, **dc dec** *(see Stitch Guide)* in next dc of same shell just worked in and 3rd dc of next shell, rep from * across, ending last rep at **, dc dec in next dc of this shell and last st, turn.

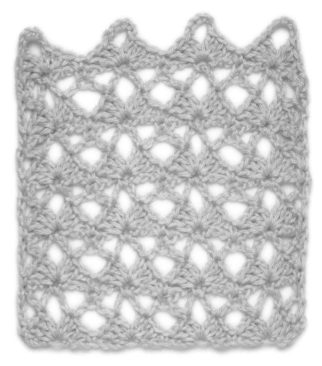

Row 3: Ch 1, sc in first st, [shell in next sc, sc in next dc dec] across, turn.

Rep rows 2 and 3 alternately for pattern. ■

#30 Flourish

PATTERN NOTES
Item shown made with size H/8/5mm crochet hook and Bernat Satin medium (worsted) weight yarn.

Pattern is worked in multiples of 12 plus 14 chains.

Chain-3 at beginning of row counts as first double crochet unless otherwise stated.

SPECIAL STITCH
Shell: (3 dc, ch 3, sc, ch 3, 3 dc) as indicated in instructions.

INSTRUCTIONS
Row 1 (WS): Sc in 2nd ch from hook, [ch 3, sk next 3 chs, sc in next ch] across, turn.

Row 2 (RS): Ch 1, sc in first st, ch 2, sc in next ch sp, *shell *(see Special Stitch)* in next ch sp, sc in next ch sp, ch 2, sc in next ch sp**, sc in next ch

sp, rep from * across, ending last rep at **, sc in last st, turn.

Row 3: Ch 3 (*see Pattern Notes*), 2 dc in next ch-2 sp, *ch 3, sc in next ch-3 sp, ch 5, sc in next ch-3 sp, ch 3**, 3 dc in next ch-2 sp, rep from * across, ending last rep at **, 2 dc in last ch-2 sp, dc in last st, turn.

Rep rows 2 and 3 alternately for pattern. ∎

#31 Stately Shells

PATTERN NOTES
Item shown made with size H/8/5mm crochet hook and Bernat Satin medium (worsted) weight yarn.

Pattern is worked in multiples of 10 plus 3 chains.

Chain-3 at beginning of row counts as first double crochet unless otherwise stated.

SPECIAL STITCH
Shell: 3 dc as indicated in instructions.

INSTRUCTIONS
Row 1 (RS): Sc in 2nd ch from hook, sc in next ch, [ch 1, sk next 3 chs, **shell** (*see Special Stitch*) in each of next 2 chs, ch 1, sk next 3 chs, sc in each of next 2 chs] across, turn.

Row 2: Ch 3 (*see Pattern Notes*), dc in next st, [ch 3, sk next 2 sts, sc in each of next 2 sts, ch 3, sk next 2 sts, dc in each of next 2 sts] across, turn.

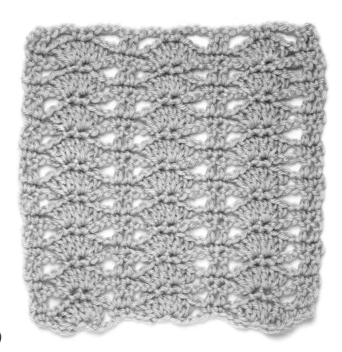

Row 3: Ch 1, sc in each of first 2 sts, [ch 1, sk next ch sp, shell in each of next 2 sts, ch 1, sk next ch sp, dc in each of next 2 sts] across, turn.

Rep rows 2 and 3 alternately for pattern. ∎

#32 Chain Reaction

PATTERN NOTES

Item shown made with size H/8/5mm crochet hook and Bernat Satin medium (worsted) weight yarn.

Pattern is worked in multiples of 6 plus 2 chains.

Chain-5 at beginning of row counts as first double crochet and chain-2 unless otherwise stated.

SPECIAL STITCH

Shell: (2 dc, ch 2, 2 dc) as indicated in instructions.

INSTRUCTIONS

Row 1 (RS): Sc in 2nd ch from hook, [sk next 2 chs, **shell** *(see Special Stitch)* in next ch, sk next 2 chs, sc in next ch] across, turn.

Row 2: Ch 5 *(see Pattern Notes)*, *sc in ch sp of next shell, ch 2, sk next 2 sts, dc in next sc**, ch 2, rep from * across, ending last rep at **, turn.

Row 3: Ch 1, sc in first st, [shell in next sc, sc in next dc] across, turn.

Row 4: Rep row 2.

Row 5: Ch 1, sc in first st, [ch 10, 2 sc in ch sp of next shell] across, ending with ch 5, **dtr** *(see Stitch Guide)* in last st, forming last ch sp, turn.

Row 6: Ch 1, sc in ch sp just formed, [ch 2, sc in next ch-10 sp] across, turn.

Row 7: Ch 1, sc in first st, [shell in next st, sc in next st] across, turn.

Rep rows 2–7 consecutively for pattern. ∎

#33 Extended Shells

PATTERN NOTES

Item shown made with size H/8/5mm crochet hook and Bernat Satin medium (worsted) weight yarn.

Pattern is worked in multiples of 6 plus 2 chains.

Chain-6 at beginning of row counts as first treble crochet and chain-2 unless otherwise stated.

SPECIAL STITCH

Extended shell (ext shell): (3 dc, ch 3, 2 dc in top of last dc worked, 3 dc) as indicated in instructions.

INSTRUCTIONS

Row 1 (RS): Sc in 2nd ch from hook, [sk next 2 chs, **ext shell** (*see Special Stitch*) in next ch, sk next 2 chs, sc in next ch] across, turn.

Row 2: Ch 6 (*see Pattern Notes*), [sc in ch-3 sp of next ext shell, ch 2, tr in next sc] across, turn.

Row 3: Ch 1, sc in first st, [ext shell in next sc, sc in next tr] across, turn.

Rep rows 2 and 3 alternately for pattern. ■

#34 Standout Shells

PATTERN NOTES

Item shown made with size H/8/5mm crochet hook and Bernat Satin medium (worsted) weight yarn.

Pattern is worked in multiples of 8 plus 2 chains.

Chain-3 at beginning of row counts as first double crochet unless otherwise stated.

SPECIAL STITCHES

Shell: (3 dc, ch 1, 3 dc) as indicated in instructions.

V-stitch (V-st): (Dc, ch 1, dc) as indicated in instructions.

INSTRUCTIONS

Row 1 (RS): Sc in 2nd ch from hook, [sk next 3 chs, **shell** *(see Special Stitches)* in next ch, sk next 3 chs, sc in next ch] across, turn.

Row 2: **Ch 3** *(see Pattern Notes)*, dc in same st as beg ch-3, [ch 1, **V-st** *(see Special Stitches)* in ch sp of next shell, ch 1, V-st in next sc] across, ending with ch 1, 2 dc in last st, turn.

Row 3: Ch 1, sc in first st, [shell in ch sp of next V-st, sc in ch sp of next V-st] across, ending with shell in last V-st, 2 dc in last st, turn.

Rep rows 2 and 3 alternately for pattern. ∎

#35 Sensational

PATTERN NOTES

Item shown made with size H/8/5mm crochet hook and Bernat Satin medium (worsted) weight yarn.

Pattern is worked in multiples of 14 plus 4 chains.

Chain-5 at beginning of row counts as first double crochet and chain-2 unless otherwise stated.

Chain-3 at beginning of row counts as first double crochet unless otherwise stated.

SPECIAL STITCHES

V-stitch (V-st): (Dc, ch 1, dc) as indicated in instructions.

Shell: (2 dc, **picot**—*see Special Stitches*, dc, ch 1, dc, picot, 2 dc) as indicated in instructions.

Picot: Ch 3, sl st in top of last dc worked.

INSTRUCTIONS

Row 1 (RS): Dc in 4th ch from hook and in each ch across, turn.

Row 2: **Ch 5** *(see Pattern Notes)*, *sk next 3 sts, **V-st** *(see Special Stitches)* in next st, ch 2**, sk next 3 sts, dc in each of next 7 sts, ch 2, rep from * across, ending last rep at **, dc in last st, turn.

Row 3: **Ch 3** *(see Pattern Notes)*, *shell *(see Special Stitches)* in ch sp of next V-st**, dc in each of next 7 dc, rep from * across, ending last rep at **, dc in last st, turn.

Row 4: Ch 5, V-st in ch sp of next shell, ch 2, *dc in each of next 7 dc, ch 2, V-st in ch sp of next shell, ch 2] across, ending with dc in last st, turn.

Rows 5 & 6: Rep rows 3 and 4.

Row 7: Ch 3, dc in each st and in each ch across, turn.

Row 8: Ch 3, dc in each of next 7 dc, [ch 2, sk next 3 dc, V-st in next dc, ch 2, sk next 3 sts, dc in each of next 7 sts] across, ending with dc in last st, turn.

Row 9: Ch 3, dc in each of next 7 dc, [shell in ch sp of next V-st, dc in each of next 7 dc] across, ending with dc in last st, turn.

Row 10: Ch 3, dc in each of next 7 dc, [ch 2, V-st in ch sp of next shell, ch 2, dc in each of next 7 sts] across, ending with dc in last st, turn.

Row 11: Rep row 9.

Row 12: Rep row 10.

Row 13: Rep row 7.

Rep rows 2–13 consecutively for pattern. ■

#36 Novelty

PATTERN NOTES
Item shown made with size H/8/5mm crochet
  hook and Bernat Satin medium (worsted)
  weight yarn.

Pattern is worked in multiples of 8 plus
  12 chains.

Chain-3 at beginning of row counts as first
  double crochet unless otherwise stated.

SPECIAL STITCHES
Shell: (2 dc, ch 1, 2 dc) as indicated in
  instructions.

Box: Ch 3, **turn**, 5 dc in next ch-3 sp, ch 3,
  dc in each of next 5 dc.

INSTRUCTIONS
Row 1 (RS): 2 dc in 4th ch from hook (*first
  3 chs count as first dc*), *ch 3, sk next 3 chs, sc in
  next ch, ch 3, sk next 3 chs**, **shell** (*see Special
  Stitches*) in next ch, rep from * across, ending
  last rep at **, 3 dc in last ch, turn.

Row 2: **Ch 3** (*see Pattern Notes*), 2 dc in same
  st as beg ch-3, *ch 3, sc in next sc, **box** (*see
  Special Stitches*)**, shell in ch sp of next shell,
  rep from * across, ending last rep at **, 3 dc in
  last st, turn.

Row 3: Ch 3, 2 dc in same st as beg ch-3, *ch 3,
  sc in ch-3 sp of next box, ch 3**, shell in ch sp of
  next shell, rep from * across, ending last rep at
  **, 3 dc in last st, turn.

Row 4: Ch 3, 2 dc in same st as beg ch-3, *ch 3,
  sc in next sc, ch 3**, shell in ch sp of next shell,
  rep from * across, ending last rep at **, 3 dc in
  last st, turn.

Row 5: Ch 3, 2 dc in same st as beg ch-3, [ch 3,
  sc in next sc, box, shell in ch sp of next shell]
  across, 3 dc in last st, turn.

Row 6: Ch 3, 2 dc in same st as beg ch-3, *ch 3,
  sc in ch-3 sp of next box, ch 3**, shell in ch sp of
  next shell, rep from * across, ending last rep at
  **, 3 dc in last st, turn.

Row 7: Ch 3, 2 dc in same st as beg ch-3, *ch 3, sc
  in next sc, ch 3**, shell in ch sp of next shell, rep
  from * across, ending last rep at **, 3 dc in last
  st, turn.

Rep rows 2–7 consecutively for pattern. ■

#37 It's A Wrap

PATTERN NOTES

Item shown made with size H/8/5mm crochet hook and Bernat Satin medium (worsted) weight yarn.

Pattern is worked in multiples of 8 plus 11 chains.

Chain-3 at beginning of row counts as first double crochet unless otherwise stated.

SPECIAL STITCHES

Shell: (3 dc, ch 1, 3 dc) as indicated in instructions.

Wrap: [Yo, insert hook around post of last dc worked, pull up lp] 3 times, yo, pull through all lps on hook.

INSTRUCTIONS

Row 1 (RS): **Shell** (*see Special Stitches*) in 7th ch from hook (*first 6 chs count as first dc and sk 3 chs*), *sk next 3 chs, dc in next ch**, **wrap** (*see Special Stitches*), sk 3 chs, shell in next ch, rep from * across, ending last rep at **, turn.

Row 2: Ch 3 (*see Pattern Notes*), *shell in ch sp of next shell**, dc in dc of wrap, rep from * across, ending last rep at **, dc in last st, turn.

Row 3: Ch 3, shell in ch sp of next shell, [sk next 3 dc of shell, dc in next dc, wrap, shell in ch sp of next shell] across, ending with dc in last st, turn.

Rep rows 2 and 3 alternately for pattern. ∎

#38 Eyelet Shells

PATTERN NOTES

Item shown made with size H/8/5mm crochet hook and Bernat Satin medium (worsted) weight yarn.

Pattern is worked in multiples of 11 plus 13 chains.

Chain-3 at beginning of row counts as first double crochet unless otherwise stated.

INSTRUCTIONS

Row 1 (RS): Dc in 4th ch from hook (*first 3 chs count as first dc*), *ch 3, sk next 3 chs, sc in next ch, ch 3, sk next 3 chs**, dc in each of next

4 chs, rep from * across, ending last rep at **, dc in last ch, turn.

Row 2: **Ch 3** (*see Pattern Notes*), dc in next dc, *ch 2, sc in next ch sp, ch 3, sc in next ch sp**, ch 2, dc in each of next 4 dc, rep from * across, ending last rep at **, dc in each of last 2 sts, turn.

Row 3: Ch 3, dc in next dc, *7 dc in next ch sp**, dc in each of next 4 dc, rep from * across, ending last rep at **, dc in each of last 2 sts, turn.

Row 4: Ch 3, dc in next dc, *ch 3, sc in center dc of next dc group, ch 3, sk next 3 dc**, dc in each of next 4 dc, rep from * across, ending last rep at **, dc in each of last 2 dc, turn.

Rep rows 2–4 consecutively for pattern. ■

#39 Grandeur

PATTERN NOTES
Item shown made with size H/8/5mm crochet hook and Bernat Satin medium (worsted) weight yarn.

Pattern is worked in multiples of 8 plus 2 chains.

Chain-4 at beginning of row counts as first double crochet and chain-1 unless otherwise stated.

Chain-3 at beginning of row counts as first double crochet unless otherwise stated.

SPECIAL STITCHES
V-stitch (V-st): (Dc, ch 3, dc) as indicated in instructions.

Picot: Ch 3, sl st in top of last dc worked.

Shell: (3 dc, picot, 4 dc, picot, 2 dc) as indicated in instructions.

INSTRUCTIONS
Row 1 (RS): Sc in 2nd ch from hook, [ch 2, sk next ch, dc in each of next 5 chs, ch 2, sk next ch, sc in next ch] across, turn.

Row 2: Ch 4 (*see Pattern Notes*), dc in same st as beg ch-4 (*V-st completed*), [ch 1, sk next 2 dc, sc in next dc, ch 1, sk next 2 dc, **V-st** (*see Special Stitches*) in next sc] across, turn.

Row 3: **Ch 3** (*see Pattern Notes*), (2 dc, **picot**— *see Special Stitches*, 2 dc) in ch sp of next V-st, *dc in next sc**, **shell** (*see Special Stitches*) in ch sp of next V-st, rep from * across, ending last rep at **, (2 dc, picot, 2 dc) in ch sp of last V-st, turn.

Row 4: Ch 3, dc in next dc, ch 3, sk next 2 dc, dc in next dc, *ch 3, sk next 2 dc and next picot**, dc in each of next 3 dc, ch 3, sk next picot and next 2 dc, dc in next dc, rep from * across, ending last rep at **, dc in each of last 2 dc, turn.

Row 5: Ch 1, sc in first dc, ch 1, [2 dc in next ch sp, 3 dc in next ch sp, ch 1, sk next dc, sc in next dc] across, turn.

Rep rows 2–5 consecutively for pattern. ■

#40 Horizons

PATTERN NOTES

Item shown made with size H/8/5mm crochet
  hook and Bernat Satin medium (worsted)
  weight yarn.

Pattern is worked in multiples of 12 plus
  11 chains.

Chain-3 at beginning of row counts as first
  half double crochet and chain-1 unless
  otherwise stated.

Chain-4 at beginning of row counts as
  first double crochet and chain-1 unless
  otherwise stated.

SPECIAL STITCH

Shell: 7 dc as indicated in instructions.

INSTRUCTIONS

Row 1 (RS): Sc in 2nd ch from hook, ch 3, sk
  next 2 chs, sc in next ch, *sk next 2 chs, **shell**
  (see Special Stitch) in next ch, sk next 2 chs, sc in
  next ch**, [ch 2, sk next ch, sc in next ch] twice,
  rep from * across, ending last rep at **, turn.

Row 2: **Ch 3** (see Pattern Notes), sc in next ch
  sp, *dc in first dc of shell, [ch 1, dc in next dc]
  6 times, sc in next ch sp**, ch 3, sc in next ch sp,
  rep from * across, ending last rep at **, ch 1, hdc
  in last st, turn.

Row 3: Ch 3 (counts as first dc), 4 dc in next ch-1
  sp, *sk next 2 ch-1 sps, sc in next ch-1 sp, ch 3,

sc in next dc, ch 3, sc in next ch-1 sp**, shell in
next ch-3 sp, rep from * across, ending last rep
at **, sk next ch-1 sp and next dc, 4 dc in last
ch-1 sp, turn.

Row 4: **Ch 4** (see Pattern Notes), dc in next dc,
[ch 1, dc in next dc] twice, *sc in next ch-3 sp,
ch 3, sc in next ch-3 sp, dc in next dc**, [ch 1,
dc in next dc] 6 times, rep from * across, ending
last rep at **, [ch 1, dc in next dc] 3 times, turn.

Row 5: Ch 1, sc in first st, ch 3, sc in next dc,
*shell in next ch-3 sp**, sk next ch-1 sp, sc in
next ch-1 sp, ch 3, sc in next dc, ch 3, sc in
next ch-1 sp, rep from * across, ending last rep
at **, sk next 2 dc, sc in next dc, ch 3, sc in last
dc, turn.

Rep rows 2–5 consecutively for pattern. ■

#41 Jazzy

PATTERN NOTES

Item shown made with size H/8/5mm crochet hook and Bernat Satin medium (worsted) weight yarn.

Pattern is worked in multiples of 9 plus 2 chains.

Chain-6 at beginning of row counts as first treble crochet and chain-2 unless otherwise stated.

Chain-4 at beginning of row counts as first treble crochet unless otherwise stated.

Chain-5 at beginning of row counts as first double crochet and chain-2 unless otherwise stated.

Chain-3 at beginning of row counts as first double crochet unless otherwise stated.

SPECIAL STITCH

V-stitch (V-st): (Dc, ch 3, dc) as indicated in instructions.

INSTRUCTIONS

Row 1 (RS): Sc in 2nd ch from hook, [ch 4, sk next 2 chs, sc in next ch] across, turn.

Row 2: Ch 6 *(see Pattern Notes)*, *sc in next ch sp, ch 2, 5 dc in next ch sp, ch 2, sc in next ch sp, ch 2, rep from * across, tr in last st, turn.

Row 3: Ch 1, sc in first st, ch 2, sk next 2 ch sps, *dc in each of next 2 dc, **V-st** *(see Special Stitch)* in next dc, dc in each of next 2 dc, ch 2**, sk next ch sp, sc in next ch sp, ch 2, sk next ch sp, rep from * across, ending last rep at **, sk last 2 ch sps, sc in last st, turn.

Row 4: Ch 4 *(see Pattern Notes)*, [**dc dec** *(see Stitch Guide)* in next 3 dc, ch 3, (2 dc, ch 1, 2 dc) in ch sp of next V-st, ch 3, dc dec in next 3 dc] across, ending with tr in last st, turn.

Row 5: Ch 5 *(see Pattern Notes)*, [sc in next ch sp, ch 2] across, dc in last st, turn.

Row 6: Ch 3 *(see Pattern Notes)*, 2 dc in next ch-2 sp, *[ch 2, sc in next ch sp] twice, ch 2**, 5 dc in next ch sp, rep from * across, ending last rep at **, 2 dc in last ch sp, dc in last st, turn.

Row 7: Ch 4 *(counts as first dc and ch-1)*, dc in same st as beg ch-4, dc in each of next 2 dc, *ch 2, sk next ch sp, sc in next ch sp, ch 2, dc in each of next 2 dc**, V-st in next dc, dc in each of next 2 dc, rep from * across, ending last rep at **, (dc, ch 1, dc) in last st, turn.

Row 8: Ch 3, 2 dc in next ch sp, ch 3, *[dc dec in next 3 dc] twice, ch 3**, (2 dc, ch 1, 2 dc) in next ch-3 sp, rep from * across, ending last rep at **, 3 dc in last st, turn.

Row 9: Ch 1, sc in first st, [ch 3, sc in next ch sp] across, turn.

Rep rows 2–9 consecutively for pattern. ∎

#42 Delicate

PATTERN NOTES
Item shown made with size H/8/5mm crochet
hook and Bernat Satin medium (worsted)
weight yarn.

Pattern is worked in multiples of 3 plus 4 chains.

Chain-3 at beginning of row counts as first
double crochet unless otherwise stated.

INSTRUCTIONS
Row 1 (RS): Dc in 4th ch from hook (*first 3 chs
count as first dc*), dc in each ch across, turn.

Row 2: Ch 6, dc in 3rd ch from hook, dc in same
st as beg ch-6, sk next 2 dc, [dc in next dc, ch 3,
dc in 3rd ch from hook, dc in same st as last dc
worked, sk next 2 dc] across, ending with dc in
last dc, turn.

Row 3: **Ch 3** (*see Pattern Notes*), 3 dc in each
ch-3 sp across, dc in last st, turn.

Rep rows 2 and 3 alternately for pattern. ■

#43 Together Again

PATTERN NOTES
Item shown made with size H/8/5mm crochet
hook and Bernat Satin medium (worsted)
weight yarn.

Pattern is worked in multiples of 4 plus
8 chains.

Chain-4 at beginning of row counts as first treble
crochet unless otherwise stated.

INSTRUCTIONS
Row 1 (RS): Dc in 4th ch from hook (*first 3 chs
count as first dc*), 2 dc in next ch, dc in next ch,
[sk next ch, dc in next ch, 2 dc in next ch, dc in
next ch] across to last 2 chs, sk next ch, dc in
last ch, turn.

Row 2: Ch 1, sc in each of first 2 dc, [ch 2, **dc dec**
(*see Stitch Guide*) in next 2 dc, ch 2, sc in each of
next 2 dc] across, turn.

Row 3: **Ch 4** (*see Pattern Notes*), [dc in next ch
sp, 2 dc in next dc dec, dc in next ch sp] across,
ending with tr in last st, turn.

Rep rows 2 and 3 alternately for pattern. ■

#44 Muddle

PATTERN NOTES

Item shown made with size H/8/5mm crochet hook and Bernat Satin medium (worsted) weight yarn.

Pattern is worked in multiples of 5 plus 2 chains.

SPECIAL STITCHES

Shell: (Sc, ch 3, 3 dc) as indicated in instructions.

Beginning cluster (beg cl): Ch 3, dc in same st as beg ch-3.

3-double crochet cluster (3-dc cl): Holding back last lp of each st on hook, 3 dc as indicated in instructions, yo, pull through all lps on hook.

2-double crochet cluster (2-dc cl): Holding back last lp of each st on hook, 2 dc as indicated in instructions, yo, pull through all lps on hook.

INSTRUCTIONS

Row 1 (RS): Shell (*see Special Stitches*) in 2nd ch from hook, sk next 4 chs, [shell in next ch, sk next 4 chs] across, ending with sc in last ch, turn.

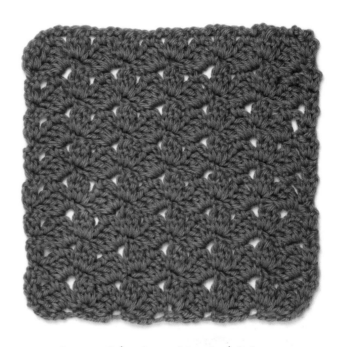

Row 2: Beg cl (*see Special Stitches*), *ch 2, sc in ch sp of next shell, ch 2**, **3-dc cl** (*see Special Stitches*) in next sc, rep from * across, ending last rep at **, **2-dc cl** (*see Special Stitches*) in last st, turn.

Row 3: Ch 1, sc in first st, 3 dc in next ch-2 sp, *sk next ch-2 sp, shell in next ch-2 sp, rep from * across, ending with sc in last st, turn.

Rep rows 2 and 3 alternately for pattern. ■

#45 Double Up

PATTERN NOTES

Item shown made with size H/8/5mm crochet hook and Bernat Satin medium (worsted) weight yarn.

Pattern is worked in multiples of 12 plus 7 chains.

Chain-3 at beginning of row counts as first double crochet unless otherwise stated.

SPECIAL STITCHES

Shell: 5 dc as indicated in instructions.

Cross stitch (cross-st): Dc in first dc of next shell, **fptr** (*see Stitch Guide*) around post of 4th dc of same shell, ch 1, **fpdc** (*see Stitch Guide*) around post of 2nd dc of same shell, dc in last dc of same shell.

INSTRUCTIONS

Row 1 (WS): Dc in 4th ch from hook (*first 3 chs count as first dc*), dc in each of next 3 chs, [ch 1, sk next 3 chs, **shell** (*see Special Stitches*) in next ch, ch 1, sk next 3 chs, dc in each of next 5 sts] across, turn.

Row 2 (RS): **Ch 3** (*see Pattern Notes*), dc in each of next 4 dc, [**cross-st** (*see Special Stitches*), ch 1, dc in each of next 5 dc] across, turn.

Row 3: Ch 3, dc in each of next 4 dc, [ch 1, shell in ch sp of next cross-st, ch 1, dc in each of next 5 dc] across, turn.

Rep rows 2 and 3 alternately for pattern. ∎

#46 Bravado

PATTERN NOTES
Item shown made with size H/8/5mm crochet hook and Bernat Satin medium (worsted) weight yarn.

Pattern is worked in multiples of 10 plus 12 chains.

Chain-4 at beginning of row counts as first treble crochet unless otherwise stated.

Chain-3 at beginning of row counts as first half double crochet and chain-1 unless otherwise stated.

Chain-5 at beginning of row counts as first double crochet and chain-2 unless otherwise stated.

SPECIAL STITCH
Shell: 9 tr as indicated in instructions.

INSTRUCTIONS
Row 1 (WS): Sc in 7th ch from hook (*first 6 chs count as first hdc, ch-3 and sk next ch*), *[ch 3, sk next ch, sc in next ch] twice**, ch 4, sc in next ch, rep from * across, ending last rep at **, ch 2, hdc in last ch, turn.

Row 2: **Ch 4** (*see Pattern Notes*), 4 tr in next ch-2 sp, *sc in next ch-3 sp, ch 3, sc in next ch-3 sp**, **shell** (*see Special Stitch*) in next ch-4 sp, rep from * across, ending last rep at **, 4 tr in last ch-2 sp, tr in last st, turn.

Row 3: Ch 1, sc in each of first 2 sts, *ch 5, (sc, ch 3, sc) in next ch-3 sp, ch 5**, sk next 3 tr of shell, sc in each of next 3 tr of same shell, rep from * across, ending last rep at **, sc in each of last 2 sts, turn.

Row 4: Ch 1, sc in first st, ch 3, sc in next ch-5 sp, *ch 4, sc in next ch-3 sp, ch 3, sk next sc, sc in next sc**, ch 3, sc in next ch-5 sp, rep from * across, ending last rep at **, turn.

Row 5: **Ch 3** (*see Pattern Notes*), *sc in next ch-3 sp, shell in next ch-4 sp, sc in next ch-3 sp**, ch 3, rep from * across, ending last rep at **, ch 1, hdc in last st, turn.

Row 6: Ch 1, sc in first st, *ch 5, sk next 3 tr of

shell, sc in each of next 3 tr of same shell, ch 5**, (sc, ch 3, sc) in next ch-3 sp, rep from * across, ending last rep at **, sc in last st, turn.

Row 7: **Ch 5** *(see Pattern Notes)*, *sc in next ch-5 sp, ch 3, sk next sc, sc in next sc, ch 3, sc in next ch-5 sp**, ch 4, rep from * across, ending last rep at **, ch 2, dc in last st, turn.

Rep rows 2–7 consecutively for pattern. ■

#47 Bumpin' Along

PATTERN NOTES

Item shown made with size H/8/5mm crochet hook and Bernat Satin medium (worsted) weight yarn.

Pattern is worked in multiples of 6 plus 7 chains.

Chain-4 at beginning of row counts as first double crochet and chain-1 unless otherwise stated.

Chain-3 at beginning of row counts as first half double crochet and chain-1 unless otherwise stated.

SPECIAL STITCHES

Shell: 5 dc as indicated in instructions.

Beginning cluster (beg cl): Ch 2, dc in same st as beg ch-2.

Cluster (cl): Holding back last lp of each st on hook, 3 dc as indicated in instructions, yo, pull through all lps on hook.

End cluster (end cl): Holding back last lp of each st on hook, 2 dc as indicated in instructions, yo, pull through all lps on hook.

INSTRUCTIONS

Row 1 (WS): Sc in 5th ch from hook *(first 4 chs count as first hdc, ch-1 and sk 1 ch)*, [ch 3, sk next 2 chs, sc in next ch] across to last 2 chs, ch 1, sk next ch, hdc in last ch, turn.

Row 2: Ch 1, sc in first st, *ch 1, **shell** *(see Special Stitches)* in next ch-3 sp, ch 1**, sc in next ch-3 sp, rep from * across, ending last rep at **, sc in last st, turn.

Row 3: **Beg cl** *(see Special Stitches)* in first st, ch 3, sk next 2 dc, sc in next dc, ch 3, [**cl** *(see Special Stitches)* in next sc, ch 3, sk next 2 dc, sc in next dc, ch 3] across, ending with **end cl** *(see Special Stitches)* in last st, turn.

Row 4: **Ch 4** *(see Pattern Notes)*, sc in next ch-3 sp, [ch 3, sc in next ch-3 sp] across, ending with ch 1, dc in last st, turn.

Row 5: **Ch 3** *(see Pattern Notes)*, 2 dc in first ch-1 sp, ch 1, sc in next ch-3 sp, [ch 1, shell in next ch-3 sp, ch 1, sc in next ch-3 sp] across, ending with 2 dc in last ch-1 sp, dc in last st, turn.

Row 6: Ch 1, sc in first st, ch 3, cl in next sc, *ch 3, sk next 2 dc, sc in next dc**, ch 3, cl in next sc, rep from * across, ending last rep at **, turn.

Row 7: Ch 4, [sc in next ch-3 sp, ch 3] across to last ch-3 sp, sc in last ch-3 sp, ch 1, dc in last st, turn.

Rep rows 2–7 consecutively for pattern. ■

#48 Hasty Lace

PATTERN NOTES
Item shown made with size H/8/5mm crochet hook and Bernat Satin medium (worsted) weight yarn.

Pattern is worked in multiples of 12 plus 2 chains.

Chain-3 at beginning of row counts as first double crochet unless otherwise stated.

SPECIAL STITCH
Shell: 6 dc as indicated in instructions.

INSTRUCTIONS
Row 1 (RS): Sc in 2nd ch from hook, [sk next 2 chs, **shell** *(see Special Stitch)* in next ch, sk next 2 chs, sc in next ch] across, turn.

Row 2: Ch 3 *(see Pattern Notes)*, **dc dec** *(see Stitch Guide)* in next 3 dc, ch 7, [dc dec in next 6 dc, ch 7] across, ending with dc dec in last 4 dc, turn.

Row 3: Ch 3, shell in 3rd ch of each ch-7 across, ending with dc in last st, turn.

Rep rows 2 and 3 alternately for pattern. ■

#49 Hugs

PATTERN NOTES
Item shown made with size H/8/5mm crochet hook and Bernat Satin medium (worsted) weight yarn.

Pattern is worked in multiples of 6 plus 7 chains.

Chain-3 at beginning of row counts as first double crochet unless otherwise stated.

SPECIAL STITCH
Shell: 3 dc as indicated in instructions.

INSTRUCTIONS
Row 1 (RS): 2 dc in 4th ch from hook *(first 3 chs count as first dc)*, sk next 2 chs, sc in next ch, [ch 3, sk next 2 chs, **shell** *(see Special Stitch)* in next ch, sk next 2 chs, sc in next ch] across, turn.

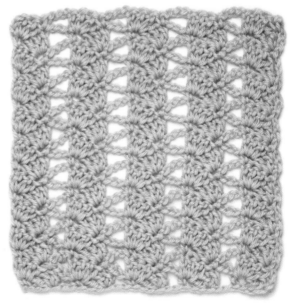

Row 2: Ch 3 *(see Pattern Notes)*, 2 dc in same st as beg ch-3, sc in 3rd dc of next shell, [ch 3, shell in next sc, ch 3, sc in 3rd dc of next shell] across, turn.

Rep row 2 for pattern. ■

#50 Mix It Up

PATTERN NOTES

Item shown made with size H/8/5mm crochet
hook and Bernat Satin medium (worsted)
weight yarn.

Pattern is worked in multiples of 8 plus
12 chains.

Chain-4 at beginning of row counts as first
double crochet and chain-1 unless otherwise
stated.

Chain-3 at beginning of row counts as first
double crochet unless otherwise stated.

SPECIAL STITCHES

Shell: (2 dc, {ch 1, 2 dc} twice) as indicated in
instructions.

V-stitch (V-st): (Dc, ch 1, dc) as indicated in
instructions.

INSTRUCTIONS

Row 1 (RS): Dc in 4th ch from hook (*first
3 chs count as first dc*), *sk next 3 chs, **shell** (*see
Special Stitches*) in next ch, sk next 3 chs**,
V-st (*see Special Stitches*) in next ch, rep from *
across, ending last rep at **, 2 dc in last ch, turn.

Row 2: Ch 4 (*see Pattern Notes*), dc in same st as
beg ch-4, *2 dc in first ch sp of next shell, ch 3,
2 dc in next ch sp of same shell**, (dc, ch 2, dc)
in ch sp of next V-st, rep from * across, ending
last rep at **, V-st in last st, turn.

Row 3: **Ch 3** (*see Pattern Notes*), dc in same st as
beg ch-3, ch 1, 2 dc in next ch-1 sp, V-st in next
ch-2 sp, *shell in next ch-2 sp, V-st in next ch-2
sp, rep from * across, 2 dc in ch-1 sp, ch 1, 2 dc
in last st, turn.

Row 4: Ch 4, 2 dc in next ch-1 sp, (dc, ch 2, dc)
in ch sp of next V-st, [2 dc in first ch sp of next
shell, ch 2, 2 dc in next ch sp of same shell, (dc,
ch 2, dc) in ch sp of next V-st] across, ending
with 2 dc in last ch sp, ch 1, dc in last st, turn.

Row 5: Ch 4, dc in same st as beg ch-3, *shell in
next ch-2 sp**, V-st in next ch-2 sp, rep from *
across, ending last rep at **, V-st in last st, turn.

Rep rows 2–5 consecutively for pattern. ■

#51 Snuggle

PATTERN NOTES

Item shown made with size H/8/5mm crochet hook and Bernat Satin medium (worsted) weight yarn.

Pattern is worked in multiples of 8 plus 2 chains.

Chain-4 at beginning of row counts as first treble crochet unless otherwise stated.

SPECIAL STITCHES

Shell: (3 dc, ch 3, 3 dc) as indicated in instructions.

Decrease (dec): Holding back last lp of each st on hook, dc in 2nd dc of next shell, tr in next sc, sk next dc, dc in next dc, yo, pull through all lps on hook.

INSTRUCTIONS

Row 1 (RS): Sc in 2nd ch from hook, [sk next 3 chs, **shell** (*see Special Stitches*) in next ch, sk next 3 chs, sc in next ch] across, turn.

Row 2: Ch 4 (*see Pattern Notes*), dc in 2nd dc of next shell, *ch 3, sc in next ch-3 sp**, ch 3, **dec**

(*see Special Stitches*), rep from * across, ending last rep at **, dc in next st, **tr dec** (*see Stitch Guide*) in same st as last dc worked and last st, turn.

Row 3: Ch 1, sc in first st, [shell in next sc, sc in next dec] across, turn.

Rep rows 2 and 3 alternately for pattern. ■

#52 Celebration

PATTERN NOTES

Item shown made with size H/8/5mm crochet hook and Bernat Satin medium (worsted) weight yarn.

Pattern is worked in multiples of 12 plus 2 chains.

Chain-3 at beginning of row counts as first double crochet unless otherwise stated.

SPECIAL STITCHES

Open shell: (Dc, {ch 1, dc} 4 times) as indicated in instructions.

Large shell (lg shell): (2 dc, ch 1, 2 dc) as indicated in instructions.

INSTRUCTIONS

Row 1 (RS): Sc in 2nd ch from hook, [ch 3, sk next 5 chs, **open shell** (*see Special Stitches*) in next ch, ch 3, sk next 5 chs, sc in next ch] across, turn.

Row 2: **Ch 3** (*see Pattern Notes*), 2 dc in same st as beg ch-3, *ch 1, sc in first ch-1 sp of open shell, [ch 3, sc in next ch-1 sp] 3 times across same open shell, ch 1**, **lg shell** (*see Special Stitches*) in next sc, ch 1, rep from * across, ending last rep at **, 3 dc in last st, turn.

Row 3: Ch 3, 2 dc in same st as beg ch-3, *ch 2, sc in next ch-3 sp, [ch 3, sc in next ch-3 sp] twice, ch 2**, lg shell in ch sp of next lg shell, rep from * across, ending last rep at **, 3 dc in last st, turn.

Row 4: Ch 3, 2 dc in same st as beg ch-3, *[ch 3, sc in next ch-3 sp] twice, ch 3**, lg shell in ch sp of next lg shell, rep from * across, ending last rep at **, 3 dc in last st, turn.

Row 5: Ch 1, sc in first st, *ch 3, sk next ch-3 sp, open shell in next ch-3 sp, ch 2**, sc in ch sp of next lg shell, ch 2, rep from * across, ending with sc in last st, turn.

Rep rows 2–5 consecutively for pattern. ■

#53 Pineapple Panels

PATTERN NOTES
Item shown made with size H/8/5mm crochet hook and Bernat Satin medium (worsted) weight yarn.

Pattern is worked in multiples of 12 plus 17 chains.

Chain-3 at beginning of row counts as first double crochet unless otherwise stated.

INSTRUCTIONS

Row 1 (WS): Dc in 4th ch from hook (*first 3 chs count as first dc*), dc in each of next 2 chs, *ch 4, sk next 2 chs, sc in next ch, ch 5, sk next 3 chs, sc in next ch, ch 4**, dc in each of next 5 chs, rep from * across, ending last rep at **, dc in each of last 4 chs, turn.

Row 2 (RS): **Ch 3** (*see Pattern Notes*), dc in each of next 3 dc, *ch 1, 9 tr in next ch-5 sp, ch 1**, dc in each of next 5 dc, rep from * across, ending last rep at **, dc in each of last 4 dc, turn.

Row 3: Ch 3, dc in each of next 3 dc, *ch 3, sc in next tr, [ch 3, sk next tr, sc in next tr] 4 times, ch 3**, dc in each of next 5 dc, rep from * across, ending last rep at **, dc in each of last 4 dc, turn.

Row 4: Ch 3, dc in each of next 3 dc, *ch 4, sk next ch-3 sp, sc in next ch-3 sp, [ch 3, sc in next ch-3 sp] 3 times, ch 3**, dc in each of next 5 dc, rep from * across, ending last rep at **, dc in each of last 4 dc, turn.

Row 5: Ch 3, dc in each of next 3 dc, *ch 4, sk next ch-4 sp, sc in next ch-3 sp, [ch 3, sc in next ch-3 sp] twice, ch 3**, dc in each of next 5 dc, rep from * across, ending last rep at **, dc in each of last 4 dc, turn.

Row 6: Ch 3, dc in each of next 3 dc, *ch 7, sk next ch-4 sp, sc in next ch-3 sp, ch 3, sc in next ch-3 sp, ch 7**, dc in each of next 5 dc, rep from

* across, ending last rep at **, dc in each of last 4 dc, turn.

Row 7: Ch 3, dc in each of next 3 dc, *ch 4, sc in next ch-7 sp, ch 5, sc in next ch-7 sp, ch 4**, dc

in each of next 5 dc, rep from * across, ending last rep at **, dc in each of last 4 dc, turn.

Rep rows 2–7 consecutively for pattern. ■

#54 Perky Posies

PATTERN NOTES
Item shown made with size H/8/5mm crochet hook and Bernat Satin medium (worsted) weight yarn.

Pattern is worked in multiples of 6 plus 9 chains.

Chain-5 at beginning of row counts as first double crochet and chain-2 unless otherwise stated.

SPECIAL STITCHES
Split decrease (split dec): Holding back last lp of each st on hook, dc in next dc, sk next 3 dc, dc in next dc, yo, pull through all lps on hook.

Picot: Ch 3, sl st in top of last st worked.

INSTRUCTIONS
Row 1 (RS): Dc in 4th ch from hook (*first 3 chs count as first dc*), dc in each st across, turn.

Row 2: Ch 5 (*see Pattern Notes*), ***split dec** (*see Special Stitches*), **picot** (*see Special Stitches*) 3 times, ch 2, dc in next dc**, ch 2, rep from * across, ending last rep at **, turn.

Row 3: Ch 5, *sk next picot, sc in next picot, ch 2, dc in next dc**, ch 2, rep from * across, ending last rep at **, turn.

Row 4: Ch 3, [2 dc in next ch-2 sp, dc in next sc, 2 dc in next ch-2 sp, dc in next dc] across, turn.

Rep rows 2–4 consecutively for pattern. ■

#55 Triad

PATTERN NOTES
Item shown made with size H/8/5mm crochet hook and Bernat Satin medium (worsted) weight yarn.

Pattern is worked in multiples of 7 plus 2 chains.

Chain-6 at beginning of row counts as first treble crochet and chain-2 unless otherwise stated.

Chain-3 at beginning of row counts as first double crochet unless otherwise stated.

SPECIAL STITCHES
Shell: 7 dc as indicated in instructions.

Cluster (cl): Holding back last lp of each st on hook, 2 dc as indicated in instructions, yo, pull through all lps on hook.

INSTRUCTIONS
Row 1: Sc in 2nd ch from hook, [ch 4, sk next 4 chs, sc in next ch, ch 2, sk next ch, sc in next ch] across, turn.

Row 2: Ch 1, sc in first st, *shell (see Special Stitches) in next ch-4 sp**, sc in next ch-2 sp, rep from * across, ending last rep at **, sc in last sc, turn.

Row 3: Ch 6 (see Pattern Notes), cl (see Special Stitches) in same st as beg ch-6, *ch 2, sk next shell**, (cl, ch 4, cl) in next sc, rep from * across, ending last rep at **, (cl, ch 1, tr) in last st, turn.

Row 4: Ch 3 (see Pattern Notes), 3 dc in next ch-1 sp, *sc in next ch-2 sp**, shell in next ch-4 sp, rep from * across, ending last rep at **, 3 dc in last ch-1 sp, dc in last st, turn.

Row 5: Ch 1, sc in first st, ch 1, *(cl, ch 4, cl) in next sc**, ch 2, rep from * across, ending last rep at **, ch 1, sc in last st, turn.

Rep rows 2–5 consecutively for pattern. ■

#56 Ovation

PATTERN NOTES
Item shown made with size H/8/5mm crochet
hook and Bernat Satin medium (worsted)
weight yarn.

Pattern is worked in multiples of 10 plus
2 chains.

Chain-3 at beginning of row counts as first
double crochet unless otherwise stated.

SPECIAL STITCH
Shell: (3 dc, ch 3, sc, ch 3, 3 dc) as indicated in
instructions.

INSTRUCTIONS
Row 1 (RS): Sc in 2nd ch from hook, [ch 2, sk
next 4 sts, **shell** (*see Special Stitch*) in next ch,
ch 2, sk next 4 chs, sc in next ch] across, turn.

Row 2: Ch 3 (*see Pattern Notes*), **dc dec** (*see
Stitch Guide*) in next 3 dc, ch 3, sc in next ch-3
sp, ch 3, sc in next ch-3 sp, *ch 3, [dc dec in next
3 dc] twice, ch 3, sc in next ch-3 sp, ch 3, sc in
next ch-3 sp, rep from * across, ending with ch
3, dc dec in next 3 sts, dc in last st, turn.

Row 3: Ch 3, 3 dc in same st as beg ch-3, ch 2,
*sk next ch sp, sc in next ch-3 sp, ch 2**, shell in
next dc dec, ch 2, rep from * across, ending last
rep at **, 4 dc in last st, turn.

Row 4: Ch 1, sc in first st, ch 3, *[dc dec in next
3 sts] twice**, [ch 3, sc in next ch-3 sp] twice,
ch 3, rep from * across, ending last rep at **,
ch 3, sc in last st, turn.

Row 5: Ch 1, sc in first st, *ch 2, shell in next
dc dec, ch 2, sk next ch sp**, sc in next ch-3 sp,
rep from * across, ending last rep at **, sc in last
st, turn.

Rep rows 2–5 consecutively for pattern. ■

#57 Springtime

PATTERN NOTES

Item shown made with size H/8/5mm crochet
   hook and Bernat Satin medium (worsted)
   weight yarn.

Pattern is worked in multiples of 6 plus
   7 chains.

Chain-3 at beginning of row counts as first
   double crochet unless otherwise stated.

SPECIAL STITCHES

V-stitch (V-st): (Dc, ch 1, dc) as indicated in
   instructions.

Beginning cluster (beg cl): Ch 2, dc in same
   st as beg ch-2.

Cluster (cl): Holding back last lp of each st on
   hook, 2 dc as indicated in instructions, yo, pull
   through all lps on hook.

Shell: (Cl, {ch 1, cl} twice) as indicated in instructions.

INSTRUCTIONS

Row 1 (RS): Dc in 4th ch from hook (*first 3 chs
   count as first dc*), [**V-st** (*see Special Stitches*) in
   next ch, ch 2, sk next 2 chs] across, 2 dc in last
   ch, turn.

Rows 2–4: Ch 3 (*see Pattern Notes*), dc in same
   st as beg ch-3, V-st in ch sp of each V-st across,
   2 dc in last st, turn.

Row 5: **Beg cl** (*see Special Stitches*), ch 2, **cl** (*see
   Special Stitches*) in same st as beg cl, [sk next
   V-st, **shell** (*see Special Stitches*) in ch sp of next
   V-st] across, (cl, ch 2, cl) in last st, turn.

Row 6: Ch 1, sc in first st, [sc in next ch-2 sp,
   ch 2] across, sc in last ch-1 sp, sc in last st, turn.

Row 7: Ch 3, dc in first st, V-st in each ch-2 sp
   across, 2 dc in last st, turn.

Rep rows 2–7 consecutively for pattern. ∎

#58 Fantastic

PATTERN NOTES
Item shown made with size H/8/5mm crochet
hook and Bernat Satin medium (worsted)
weight yarn.

Pattern is worked in multiples of 8 plus 2 chains.

Chain-4 at beginning of row counts as first double
crochet and chain-1 unless otherwise stated.

Chain-3 at beginning of row counts as first
double crochet unless otherwise stated.

SPECIAL STITCHES
Shell: 9 dc as indicated in instructions.

V-stitch (V-st): (Dc, ch 2, dc) as indicated in
instructions.

INSTRUCTIONS
Row 1 (RS): Sc in 2nd ch from hook, [sk next
3 chs, **shell** (*see Special Stitches*) in next ch, sk
next 3 chs, sc in next ch] across, turn.

Row 2: Ch 4 (*see Pattern Notes*), dc in same st as
beg ch-4, [ch 2, sk next 4 dc, sc in next dc, ch 2,
sk next 4 dc, **V-st** (*see Special Stitches*) in next
sc] across, turn.

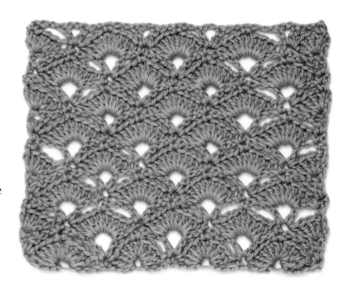

Row 3: Ch 3 (*see Pattern Notes*), 4 dc in same st
as beg ch-3, sc in next sc, [shell in ch sp of next
V-st, sc in next sc] across, 5 dc in last sc, turn.

Row 4: Ch 1, sc in first st, ch 2, *V-st in next sc,
ch 2, sk next 4 dc, sc in next dc**, ch 2, rep from
* across, ending last rep at **, turn.

Row 5: Ch 1, sc in first st, [shell in ch sp of next
V-st, sc in next sc] across, turn.

Rep rows 2–5 consecutively for pattern. ∎

#59 Debonair

PATTERN NOTES
Item shown made with size H/8/5mm crochet
hook and Bernat Satin medium (worsted)
weight yarn.

Pattern is worked in multiples of 8 plus
4 chains.

Chain-3 at beginning of row counts as first
double crochet unless otherwise stated.

SPECIAL STITCH
Shell: (4 dc, ch 1, dc) as indicated in
instructions.

INSTRUCTIONS

Row 1 (RS): Dc in 4th ch from hook (*first 3 chs count as first dc*), [sk next 3 chs, **shell** (*see Special Stitch*) in next ch, sk next 3 chs, 2 dc in next ch, mark sp between last 2 dc] across, turn.

Row 2: Ch 3 (*see Pattern Notes*), dc in same st as beg ch-3, *shell in ch sp of next shell**, 2 dc in marked sp, rep from * across, ending last rep at **, 2 dc in last st, turn.

Rep row 2 for pattern. ∎

#60 Zippity

PATTERN NOTES

Item shown made with size H/8/5mm crochet hook and Bernat Satin medium (worsted) weight yarn.

Pattern is worked in multiples of 4 plus 8 chains.

Chain-3 at beginning of row counts as first double crochet unless otherwise stated.

INSTRUCTIONS

Row 1 (RS): 2 dc in 5th ch from hook (*first 4 chs count as first dc and sk 1 ch*), 2 dc in next ch, [sk next 2 chs, 2 dc in each of next 2 chs] across to last 2 chs, sk next ch, dc in last ch, turn.

Row 2: Ch 3 (*see Pattern Notes*), sk next 4 dc, tr in sp between last sk dc and next dc, ch 2, tr in sp between first 2 sts, [sk next 4 dc, tr in sp between last sk dc and next dc, ch 2, tr in sp before first sk dc] across, dc in last st, turn.

Row 3: Ch 3, 4 dc in each ch-2 sp across, dc in last st, turn.

Rep rows 2 and 3 alternately for pattern. ∎

#61 Memory

PATTERN NOTES

Item shown made with size H/8/5mm crochet hook and Bernat Satin medium (worsted) weight yarn.

Pattern is worked in multiples of 16 plus 7 chains.

Chain-3 at beginning of row counts as first double crochet unless otherwise stated.

SPECIAL STITCH

Shell: 7 dc as indicated in instructions.

INSTRUCTIONS

Row 1 (RS): Dc in 4th ch from hook (*first 3 chs count as first dc*), *[ch 3, sk next 3 chs, sc in next ch] twice, ch 3, sk next 3 chs, dc in each of next 5 chs, rep from * across, turn.

Row 2: Ch 3 (*see Pattern Notes*), dc in each of next 4 dc, [ch 3, sc in next ch sp, **shell** (*see Special Stitch*) in next ch sp, sc in next ch sp, ch 3, dc in each of next 5 dc] across, turn.

Row 3: Ch 3, dc in each of next 4 dc, *ch 1, sc in next ch sp, dc in first dc of next shell, [ch 1, dc in next dc of same shell] 6 times, sc in next ch sp, ch 1, dc in each of next 5 dc, rep from * across, turn.

Row 4: Ch 3, dc in each dc and in each ch-1 sp across, turn.

Row 5: Ch 3, dc in each of next 4 dc, [ch 3, sk next 4 dc, sc in next dc, ch 3, sk next 3 dc, sc in next dc, ch 3, sk next 4 dc, dc in each of next 5 dc] across, turn.

Rep rows 2–5 consecutively for pattern. ∎

#62 Carefree

PATTERN NOTES

Item shown made with size H/8/5mm crochet hook and Bernat Satin medium (worsted) weight yarn.

Pattern is worked in multiples of 10 plus 2 chains.

Chain-5 at beginning of row counts as first double crochet and chain-2 unless otherwise stated.

Chain-3 at beginning of row counts as first double crochet unless otherwise stated.

INSTRUCTIONS

Row 1 (RS): Sc in 2nd ch from hook, [ch 3, sk next 2 chs, dc in each of next 5 chs, ch 3, sk next 2 chs, sc in next ch] across, turn.

Row 2: Ch 5 (*see Pattern Notes*), [sc in each of next 5 dc, ch 2, dc in next sc, ch 2] across, dc in last st, turn.

Row 3: Ch 3 (*see Pattern Notes*), 2 dc in next ch sp, *ch 3, sc in 3rd dc of next dc group, ch 3, 2 dc in next ch sp**, dc in next dc, 2 dc in next ch sp, rep from * across, ending last rep at **, dc in last st, turn.

Row 4: Ch 1, sc in each of first 3 dc, *ch 2, dc in next sc, ch 2**, sc in each of next 5 dc, rep from * across, ending last rep at **, sc in each of last 3 dc, turn.

Row 5: Ch 1, sc in first st, *ch 3, 2 dc in next ch sp, dc in next dc, 2 dc in next ch sp, ch 3, sk next 2 sc, sc in next sc, rep from * across, turn.

Rep rows 2–5 consecutively for pattern. ∎

#63 Stately

PATTERN NOTES

Item shown made with size H/8/5mm crochet hook and Bernat Satin medium (worsted) weight yarn.

Pattern is worked in multiples of 11 plus 5 chains.

Chain-3 at beginning of row counts as first double crochet unless otherwise stated.

INSTRUCTIONS

Row 1 (RS): Dc in 4th ch from hook (*first 3 chs count as first dc*), dc in each ch across, turn.

Row 2: Ch 3 (*see Pattern Notes*), dc in each of next 2 dc, [ch 3, sk next 2 dc, tr in each of next 4 dc, ch 3, dc in each of next 3 dc] across, turn.

Row 3: Ch 3, dc in each of next 2 dc, [ch 3, sc in each of next 4 tr, ch 3, dc in each of next 3 dc] across, turn.

Rows 4 & 5: Ch 3, dc in each of next 2 dc, [ch 3, sc in each of next 4 sc, ch 3, dc in each of next 3 dc] across, turn.

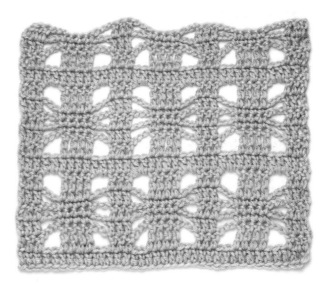

Row 6: Ch 3, dc in each of next 2 dc, [ch 3, tr in each of next 4 sc, ch 3, dc in each of next 3 dc] across, turn.

Row 7: Ch 3, dc in each st across with 2 dc in each ch sp, turn.

Rep rows 2–7 consecutively for pattern. ∎

#64 No-Brainer

PATTERN NOTES
Item shown made with size H/8/5mm crochet hook and Bernat Satin medium (worsted) weight yarn.

Pattern is worked in multiples of 2 plus 6 chains.

Chain-3 at beginning of row counts as first double crochet unless otherwise stated.

INSTRUCTIONS
Row 1 (RS): 2 dc in 4th ch from hook (*first 3 chs count as first dc*), [sk next ch, 2 dc in next ch] across to last 2 chs, sk next ch, dc in last ch, turn.

Row 2: Ch 3 (*see Pattern Notes*), [2 dc in sp between next 2 dc] across, dc in last st, turn.

Rep row 2 for pattern. ■

#65 Vamp

PATTERN NOTES
Item shown made with size H/8/5mm crochet hook and Bernat Satin medium (worsted) weight yarn.

Pattern is worked in multiples of 4 plus 3 chains.

Chain-3 at beginning of row counts as first double crochet unless otherwise stated.

SPECIAL STITCH
V-stitch (V-st): (Dc, ch 1, dc) as indicated in instructions.

INSTRUCTIONS
Row 1 (RS): Dc in 4th ch from hook (*first 3 chs count as first dc*) and in each ch across, turn.

Row 2: Ch 3 (*see Pattern Notes*), [sk next st, **V-st** (*see Special Stitch*) in next st, sk next st, dc in next st] across, turn.

Row 3: Ch 3, dc in same st as beg ch-3, *dc in ch sp of next V-st**, sk last dc of V-st, V-st in next

dc, rep from * across, ending last rep at **, 2 dc in last st, turn.

Row 4: Ch 3, sk next st, *V-st in next st**, dc in ch sp of next V-st, sk next st of V-st, rep from * across, ending last rep at **, dc in last dc, turn.

Row 5: Ch 1, dc in each st and in each ch sp across, turn.

Rep rows 2–5 consecutively for pattern. ■

#66 Double Take

PATTERN NOTES

Item shown made with size H/8/5mm crochet hook and Bernat Satin medium (worsted) weight yarn.

Pattern is worked in multiples of 8 plus 7 chains.

Chain-3 at beginning of row counts as first double crochet unless otherwise stated.

SPECIAL STITCHES

V-stitch (V-st): (Dc, ch 1, dc) as indicated in instructions.

Shell: 5 dc as indicated in instructions.

INSTRUCTIONS

Row 1 (RS): Dc in 4th ch from hook (*first 3 chs count as first dc*) and in each ch across, turn.

Row 2: Ch 3 (*see Pattern Notes*), sk next dc, **V-st** (*see Special Stitches*) in next dc, [sk next 3 dc,

shell (*see Special Stitches*) in next dc, sk next 3 dc, V-st in next dc] across to last 2 dc, sk next dc, dc in last dc, turn.

Row 3: Ch 3, dc in each st across, turn.

Rep rows 2 and 3 alternately for pattern. ■

#67 Bountiful

PATTERN NOTES

Item shown made with size H/8/5mm crochet hook and Bernat Satin medium (worsted) weight yarn.

Pattern is worked in multiples of 8 plus 2 chains.

Chain-4 at beginning of row counts as first double crochet and chain-1 unless otherwise stated.

Chain-6 at beginning of row counts as first double crochet and chain-3 unless otherwise stated.

Chain-3 at beginning of row counts as first double crochet unless otherwise stated.

SPECIAL STITCH

Shell: (3 dc, ch 2, 3 dc) as indicated in instructions.

INSTRUCTIONS

Row 1 (RS): Dc in 4th ch from hook (*first 3 chs count as first dc*) and in each ch across, turn.

Row 2: Ch 4 (*see Pattern Notes*), sk next st, dc in next st, [ch 1, sk next st, dc in next st] across, turn.

Row 3: Ch 1, sc in first st, [sk next ch sp, next dc and next ch sp, **shell** (*see Special Stitch*) in next dc, sk next ch sp, next dc and next ch sp, dc in next st] across, turn.

Row 4: **Ch 6** (*see Pattern Notes*), *sc in ch sp of next shell, ch 3, sk next 3 dc of shell, dc in next dc**, ch 3, rep from * across, ending last rep at **, turn.

Row 5: Ch 4, [dc in next ch sp, ch 1, dc in next sc, ch 1, dc in next ch sp, ch 1, dc in next dc] across, turn.

Row 6: **Ch 3** (*see Pattern Notes*), dc in each st and in each ch sp across, turn.

Row 7: Ch 3, dc in each st across, turn.

Rep rows 2–7 consecutively for pattern. ∎

#68 Sedate

PATTERN NOTES
Item shown made with size H/8/5mm crochet hook and Bernat Satin medium (worsted) weight yarn.

Pattern is worked in multiples of 8 plus 14 chains.

Chain-3 at beginning of row counts as first double crochet unless otherwise stated.

INSTRUCTIONS
Row 1 (RS): Dc in 4th ch from hook (*first 3 chs count as first dc*), [ch 2, sk next 2 chs, dc in each of next 2 chs] across, turn.

Row 2: Ch 1, sc in first st, ch 2, sc in next ch sp, [ch 3, sc in next ch sp] across, ending with ch 2, sc in last st, turn.

Row 3: **Ch 3** (*see Pattern Notes*), 3 dc in next ch-2 sp, sc in next ch-3 sp, [6 dc in next ch-3 sp, sc in next ch-3 sp] across, ending with 3 dc in last ch-2 sp, dc in last st, turn.

Row 4: Ch 3, dc in next dc, *ch 2, sk next 2 dc, 2 dc in next sc**, ch 2, sk next 2 dc, dc in each of next 2 dc, rep from * across, ending last rep at **, turn.

Rep rows 2–4 consecutively for pattern. ∎

#69 Jaunty

PATTERN NOTES

Item shown made with size H/8/5mm crochet hook and Bernat Satin medium (worsted) weight yarn.

Pattern is worked in multiples of 8 plus 11 chains.

Chain-3 at beginning of row counts as first double crochet unless otherwise stated.

INSTRUCTIONS

Row 1 (RS): 2 dc in 4th ch from hook (*first 3 chs count as first dc*), *sk next 2 chs, dc in each of next 2 chs, sk next 2 chs**, 3 dc in each of next 2 chs, rep from * across, ending last rep at **, 3 dc in last ch, turn.

Row 2: Ch 3 (*see Pattern Notes*), sk next 2 dc, *3 dc in each of next 2 dc, sk next 2 dc**, dc in each of next 2 dc, sk next 2 dc] across, dc in last dc, turn.

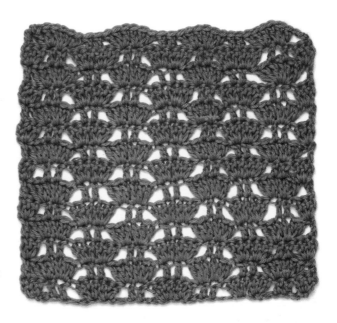

Row 3: Ch 3, 2 dc in same st as beg ch-3, *sk next 2 dc, dc in each of next 2 dc, sk next 2 dc**, 3 dc in each of next 2 dc, rep from * across, ending last rep at **, 3 dc in last st, turn.

Rep rows 2 and 3 alternately for pattern. ■

#70 Trellis Shells

PATTERN NOTES

Item shown made with size H/8/5mm crochet hook and Bernat Satin medium (worsted) weight yarn.

Pattern is worked in multiples of 12 plus 2 chains.

Chain-5 at beginning of row counts as first double crochet and chain-2 unless otherwise stated.

SPECIAL STITCH

Shell: (3 dc, ch 3, 3 dc) as indicated in instructions.

INSTRUCTIONS

Row 1 (RS): Sc in 2nd ch from hook, [ch 4, sk next 3 chs, sc in next ch] across, turn.

Row 2: **Ch 5** (*see Pattern Notes*), sc in next ch-4 sp, **shell** (*see Special Stitch*) in next ch-4 sp, ch 4, sc in next ch-4 sp] across, ending with ch 2, dc in last st, turn.

Row 3: Ch 1, sc in first st, *ch 4, (sc, ch 4, sc) in ch sp of next shell, ch 4**, sc in next ch-4 sp, rep from * across, ending last rep at **, sc in last st, turn.

Rep rows 2 and 3 alternately for pattern. ∎

#71 Victory

PATTERN NOTES
Item shown made with size H/8/5mm crochet hook and Bernat Satin medium (worsted) weight yarn.

Pattern is worked in multiples of 10 plus 15 chains.

Chain-3 at beginning of row counts as first double crochet unless otherwise stated.

Chain-4 at beginning of row counts as first double crochet and chain-1 unless otherwise stated.

SPECIAL STITCH
V-stitch (V-st): (Dc, ch 3, dc) as indicated in instructions.

INSTRUCTIONS
Row 1 (RS): Dc in 4th ch from hook (*first 3 chs count as first dc*), dc in next ch, *sk next 2 chs, **V-st** (*see Special Stitch*) in next ch, sk next 2 chs**, dc in each of next 5 chs, rep from * across, ending last rep at **, sk next 2 chs, dc in each of last 3 chs, turn.

Row 2: Ch 3 (*see Pattern Notes*), sk next dc, dc in next dc, *ch 2, 5 dc in next ch sp, ch 2, **dc dec** (*see Stitch Guide*) in first and last st of next dc group, rep from * across, turn.

Row 3: Ch 4 (*see Pattern Notes*), dc in same st as beg ch-4, *dc in each of next 5 dc**, V-st in sp

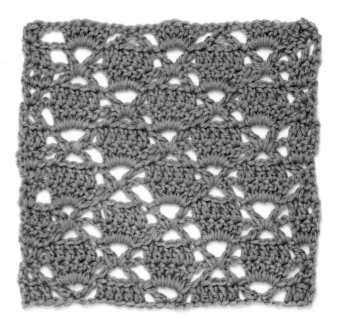

between dc of next dc dec, rep from * across, ending last rep at **, (dc, ch 1, dc) in last st, turn.

Row 4: Ch 3, 2 dc in next ch-1 sp, ch 2, dc dec in first and last dc of next dc group, ch 2**, 5 dc in ch sp of next V-st, rep from * across, ending last rep at **, 2 dc in next ch-1 sp, dc in last st, turn.

Row 5: Ch 3, dc in each of next 2 dc, *V-st in sp between dc of next dc dec**, dc in each of next 5 dc, rep from * across, ending last rep at **, dc in each of last 3 sts, turn.

Rep rows 2–5 consecutively for pattern. ∎

#72 Adventure

PATTERN NOTES
Item shown made with size H/8/5mm crochet
  hook and Bernat Satin medium (worsted)
  weight yarn.

Pattern is worked in multiples of 8 plus
  11 chains.

Chain-3 at beginning of row counts as first
  double crochet unless otherwise stated.

INSTRUCTIONS
Row 1 (RS): 2 dc in 6th ch from hook (*first
  5 chs count as first dc and sk 2 chs*), ch 5, 2 dc in
  next ch, *sk next 2 chs, dc in each of next 2 chs,
  2 dc sk next 2 chs, 2 dc in next ch, ch 5, 2 dc in
  next ch, rep from * across, sk next 2 chs, dc in
  last ch, turn.

Row 2: Ch 3 (*see Pattern Notes*), dc in each of
  next 2 dc, *2 sc in next ch-5 sp**, dc in each of
  next 6 dc, rep from * across, ending last rep at
  **, dc in each of last 3 dc, turn.

Row 3: Ch 3, *2 dc in next sc, ch 5, 2 dc in next
  sc, sk next 2 dc**, dc in each of next 2 dc, rep
  from * across, ending last rep at **, dc in last
  st, turn.

Rep rows 2 and 3 alternately for pattern. ■

#73 Spires

PATTERN NOTES
Item shown made with size H/8/5mm crochet
  hook and Bernat Satin medium (worsted)
  weight yarn.

Pattern is worked in multiples of 7 plus 8 chains.

Chain-5 at beginning of row counts as
  first double crochet and chain-2 unless otherwise stated.

SPECIAL STITCH
Shell: 6 dc as indicated in instructions.

INSTRUCTIONS
Row 1: Sc in 2nd ch from hook, *sk next 2 chs,
  shell (*see Special Stitch*) in next ch**, sk next 2
  chs, sc in each of next 2 chs, rep from * across,
  ending last rep at **, sc in last ch, turn.

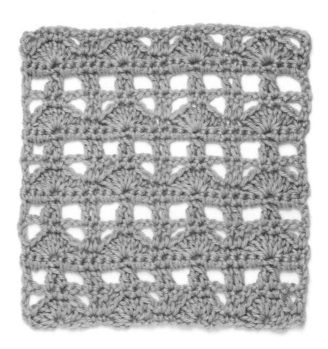

Row 2: Ch 5 (*see Pattern Note*), *sk first 2 dc of
  next shell, sc in each of next 2 dc of same shell,

ch 2, sk last 2 dc of same shell**, dc in each of next 2 sc, ch 2, rep from * across, ending last rep at **, dc in last st, turn.

Row 3: Ch 5, *dc dec *(see Stitch Guide)* in next 2 sc, ch 2**, dc in each of next 2 dc, rep from * across, ending last rep at **, dc in last st, turn.

Row 4: Ch 1, sc in first st, *2 sc in next ch-2 sp, sc in next dc dec, 2 sc in next ch-2 sp**, sc in each

of next 2 dc, rep from * across, ending last rep at **, sc in last st, turn.

Row 5: Ch 1, sc in first st, *sk next 2 sts, shell in next st, sk next 2 sts**, sc in each of next 2 sts, rep from * across, ending last rep at **, sc in last st, turn.

Rep rows 2–5 consecutively for pattern. ∎

#74 Full-Blown

PATTERN NOTES
Item shown made with size H/8/5mm crochet hook and Bernat Satin medium (worsted) weight yarn.

Pattern is worked in multiples of 10 plus 9 chains.

Chain-5 at beginning of row counts as first double crochet and chain-2 unless otherwise stated.

Chain-3 at beginning of row counts as first double crochet unless otherwise stated.

SPECIAL STITCHES
Shell: 5 dc as indicated in instructions.

V-stitch (V-st): (Dc, ch 1, dc) as indicated in instructions.

INSTRUCTIONS
Row 1 (RS): Shell *(see Special Stitches)* in 6th ch from hook *(first 5 chs count as first dc and sk 2 chs)*, *sk next 2 chs, dc in next ch**, sk next 2 chs, **V-st** *(see Special Stitches)* in next ch, sk next 2 chs, dc in next ch, sk next 2 chs, shell in next ch, rep from * across, ending last rep at **, turn.

Row 2: Ch 5 *(see Pattern Notes)*, *dc dec *(see Stitch Guide)* in next 5 dc, ch 2, dc in next dc**, ch 2, V-st in ch sp of next V-st, ch 2, dc in next dc, rep from * across, ending last rep at **, turn.

Row 3: Ch 3 *(see Pattern Notes)*, *shell in next dc dec, dc in next dc**, V-st in ch sp of next V-st, dc in next dc, rep from * across, ending last rep at **, turn.

Rep rows 2 and 3 alternately for pattern. ∎

#75 Holland's Pride

PATTERN NOTES

Item shown made with size H/8/5mm crochet hook and Bernat Satin medium (worsted) weight yarn.

Pattern is worked in multiples of 10 plus 12 chains.

Chain-4 at beginning of row counts as first double crochet and chain-1 unless otherwise stated.

Chain-3 at beginning of row counts as first double crochet unless otherwise stated.

Chain-7 at beginning of row counts as first double crochet and chain-4 unless otherwise stated.

SPECIAL STITCH

Shell: 7 dc as indicated in instructions.

INSTRUCTIONS

Row 1: Dc in 12th ch from hook (*first 11 chs count as first dc, ch-4 and sk 4 chs*), [ch 4, sk next 4 chs, dc in next ch] across, turn.

Row 2: Ch 4 (*see Pattern Notes*), *shell (*see Special Stitch*) in next dc**, ch 2, sk next dc, rep from * across, ending last rep at **, ch 1, dc in last st, turn.

Row 3: Ch 4, *dc in each of first 3 dc of next shell, ch 2, sk next dc, dc in each of last 3 dc of

same shell**, ch 2, rep from * across, ending last rep at **, ch 1, dc in last st, turn.

Row 4: Ch 3 (*see Pattern Notes*), [**dc dec** (*see Stitch Guide*) in next 3 sts, ch 3, dc in next ch-2 sp, ch 3, dc dec in next 3 sts] across, dc in last st, turn.

Row 5: Ch 7 (*see Pattern Notes*), *dc in next dc, ch 4**, dc in next ch-1 sp, ch 4, rep from * across, ending last rep at **, dc in last st, turn.

Rep rows 2–5 consecutively for pattern. ■

#76 Simple Wraps

PATTERN NOTES

Item shown made with size H/8/5mm crochet hook and Bernat Satin medium (worsted) weight yarn.

Pattern is worked in multiples of 3 plus 6 chains.

Chain-3 at beginning of row counts as first double crochet unless otherwise stated.

INSTRUCTIONS

Row 1: Dc in 4th ch from hook (*first 3 chs count as first dc*), dc in next ch, dc around posts of last 2 dc, [sk next ch, dc in each of next 2 chs, dc around posts of last 2 dc worked] across, dc in last st, turn.

Row 2: Ch 3 (*see Pattern Notes*), dc in each st across, turn.

Row 3: Ch 3, [dc in each of next 2 dc, dc around posts of last 2 dc worked] across, dc in last st, turn.

Rep rows 2 and 3 alternately for pattern. ■

#77 Tilt Columns

PATTERN NOTES

Item shown made with size H/8/5mm crochet hook and Bernat Satin medium (worsted) weight yarn.

Pattern is worked in multiples of 8 plus 5 chains.

Chain-3 at beginning of row counts as first double crochet unless otherwise stated.

INSTRUCTIONS

Row 1 (RS): Dc in 4th ch from hook (*first 3 chs count as first dc*), dc in next ch, [sk next 2 chs, dc in next ch, ch 3, 3 dc around post of last dc worked, sk next 2 chs, dc in each of next 3 chs] across, turn.

Row 2: Ch 3 (*see Pattern Notes*), dc in each of next 2 dc, [ch 2, sc in next ch-3 sp, ch 2, dc in each of next 3 dc] across, turn.

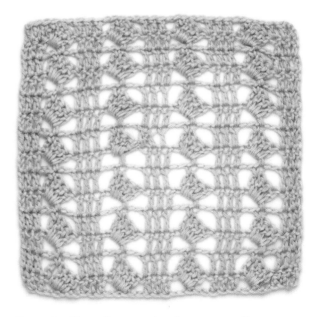

Row 3: Ch 3, dc in each of next 2 dc, [dc in next sc, ch 3, 3 dc around post of last dc worked, dc in each of next 3 dc] across, turn.

Rep rows 2 and 3 alternately for pattern. ■

#78 Alliance

PATTERN NOTES

Item shown made with size H/8/5mm crochet hook and Bernat Satin medium (worsted) weight yarn.

Pattern is worked in multiples of 10 plus 14 chains.

Chain-3 at beginning of row counts as first double crochet unless otherwise stated.

SPECIAL STITCHES

Shell: (Sc, ch 3, 3 dc) as indicated in instructions.

V-stitch (V-st): (Dc, ch 1, dc) as indicated in instructions.

INSTRUCTIONS

Row 1: Dc in 4th ch from hook (*first 3 chs count as first dc*), *ch 3, sk next 4 chs, **shell** (*see Special Stitches*) in next ch, sk next 4 chs**, **V-st** (*see Special Stitches*) in next ch, rep from * across, ending last rep at **, 2 dc in last ch, turn.

Row 2: **Ch 3** (*see Pattern Notes*), dc in same st as beg ch-3, *ch 3, shell in next ch-3 sp**, V-st in ch sp of next V-st, rep from * across, ending last rep at **, turn.

Rep row 2 for pattern. ■

#79 Baroque

PATTERN NOTES

Item shown made with size H/8/5mm crochet hook and Bernat Satin medium (worsted) weight yarn.

Pattern is worked in multiples of 8 plus 4 chains.

Chain-3 at beginning of row counts as first double crochet unless otherwise stated.

SPECIAL STITCH

Shell: (Dc, ch 3, 3 dc) around post of last dc worked.

INSTRUCTIONS

Row 1 (RS): Dc in 4th ch from hook (*first 3 chs count as first dc*), [sk next 2 chs, **shell**

(*see Special Stitch*) in next ch, sk next 3 chs, dc in each of next 2 chs] across, turn.

Row 2: **Ch 3** (*see Pattern Notes*), dc in next dc, [ch 3, sc in next ch-3 sp, 3 dc in each of next 2 dc, sc in next ch-3 sp, ch 3, dc in each of next 2 dc] across, turn.

Row 3: Ch 3, dc in next st, *shell in next sc, [**dc dec** (*see Stitch Guide*) in next 3 dc] twice, shell in next sc, dc in each of next 2 dc, rep from * across, turn.

Row 4: Ch 3, dc in next dc, [ch 3, sc in next ch-3 sp, ch 3, dc in each of next 2 dc] across, turn.

Row 5: Ch 3, dc in next dc, [shell in next sc, dc in each of next 2 dc] across, turn.

Rep rows 2–5 consecutively for pattern. ■

#80 Banter

PATTERN NOTES
Item shown made with size H/8/5mm crochet hook and Bernat Satin medium (worsted) weight yarn.

Pattern is worked in multiples of 3 plus 6 chains.

Chain-3 at beginning of row counts as first double crochet unless otherwise stated.

Chain-4 at beginning of row counts as first double crochet and chain-1 unless otherwise stated.

INSTRUCTIONS
Row 1 (RS): 3 dc in 5th ch from hook (*first 4 chs count as first dc and ch-1*), [sk next 2 chs, 3 dc in next ch] across to last 2 chs, turn.

Row 2: **Ch 3** (*see Pattern Notes*), [sk next 2 dc, dc in next dc, ch 1, dc in first sk dc] across, ending with dc in last st, turn.

Row 3: **Ch 4** (*see Pattern Notes*), [dc dec in next dc, next ch-1 and next dc, ch 2] across, turn.

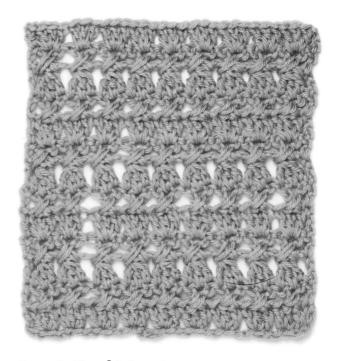

Row 4: Ch 3, [sk first ch-2 sp, dc in next ch-2 sp, ch 1, dc in ch-2 sp just sk] across, ending with dc in last st, turn.

Row 5: Ch 3, 3 dc in each ch-1 sp across, ending with dc in last st, turn.

Rep rows 2–5 consecutively for pattern. ■

#81 Sassy Shells

PATTERN NOTES

Item shown made with size H/8/5mm crochet
   hook and Bernat Satin medium (worsted)
   weight yarn.

Pattern is worked in multiples of 7 plus
   11 chains.

Chain-3 at beginning of row counts as first
   double crochet unless otherwise stated.

SPECIAL STITCH

Shell: 7 dc as indicated in instructions.

INSTRUCTIONS

Row 1: Dc in 5th ch from hook (*first 4 chs count as
   first dc and ch-1*), *sk next 2 chs, dc in next ch**,
   sk next 3 chs, dc in next ch, ch 1, dc in first sk ch
   of last 3-sk chs, rep from * across, ending last rep
   at **, sk next 2 chs, (dc, ch 1, dc) in next ch, turn.

Row 2: **Ch 3** (*see Pattern Notes*), 3 dc in next ch-1
   sp, sc in next dc, [**shell** (*see Special Stitch*) in
   next ch-1 sp, sc in next dc] across ending with
   3 dc in last ch-1 sp, dc in last st, turn.

Row 3: Ch 1, sc in each of first 2 sts, ch 2, dc in
   next sc, [ch 1, sk next 2 dc, sc in each of next

3 dc, ch 1, dc in next sc] across, ending last rep
   at ch 1, sc in each of last 2 sts, turn.

Row 4: Ch 3, *sk next ch-1 sp, dc in next ch-1
   sp, ch 1, dc in ch-1 sp just sk**, sk next sc, dc in
   next sc, rep from * across, ending last rep at **,
   dc in last st, turn.

Row 5: Ch 1, sc in first st, [shell in next ch-1 sp,
   sk next dc, sc in next dc] across, turn.

Rep rows 2–5 consecutively for pattern. ■

#82 Tête-à-Tête

PATTERN NOTES

Item shown made with size H/8/5mm crochet hook and Bernat Satin medium (worsted) weight yarn.

Pattern is worked in multiples of 4 plus 6 chains.

Chain-3 at beginning of row counts as first double crochet unless otherwise stated.

SPECIAL STITCHES

Shell: (Sc, ch 4, **puff st**—*see Special Stitches*) as indicated in instructions.

Puff stitch (puff st): Yo, insert hook in sc, yo, pull lp through, [yo, insert hook in same sc, yo, pull lp through] twice, yo, pull through all lps on hook.

INSTRUCTIONS

Row 1 (RS): Shell *(see Special Stitches)* in 2nd ch from hook, [sk next 3 chs, shell in next ch] across to last 4 chs, sk next 3 chs, sc in last ch, turn.

Row 2: Ch 3 *(see Pattern Notes)*, dc in same st as beg ch-3, 4 dc in each sc across to last sc, 3 dc in last sc, turn.

Row 3: Ch 1, shell in first st, shell in 2nd dc of each dc group across, ending with sc in last st, turn.

Rep rows 2 and 3 alternately for pattern. ∎

#83 Tempo

PATTERN NOTES

Item shown made with size H/8/5mm crochet hook and Bernat Satin medium (worsted) weight yarn.

Pattern is worked in multiples of 3 plus 7 chains.

Chain-3 at beginning of row counts as first double crochet unless otherwise stated.

SPECIAL STITCHES

Shell: (Sc, ch 4, **puff st**—*see Special Stitches*) as indicated in instructions.

Puff stitch (puff st): Yo, insert hook in sc, yo, pull lp through, [yo, insert hook in same sc, yo, pull lp through] twice, yo, pull through all lps on hook.

INSTRUCTIONS

Row 1 (WS): Dc in 4th ch from hook (*first 3 chs count as first dc*) and in each ch across, turn.

Row 2: Ch 1, sc in first st, [**shell** (*see Special Stitches*) in next st, sk next 2 sts] across, sc in last st, turn.

Row 3: Ch 3 (*see Pattern Notes*), 3 dc in ch sp of each shell across, ending with dc in last st, turn.

Row 4: Ch 3, [sk next dc, dc in each of next 2 dc, dc in dc just sk] across, dc in last st, turn.

Row 5: Ch 3, dc in each dc across, turn.

Rep rows 2–5 consecutively for pattern. ■

#84 Little Blooms

PATTERN NOTES

Item shown made with size H/8/5mm crochet hook and Bernat Satin medium (worsted) weight yarn.

Pattern is worked in multiples of 4 plus 7 chains.

Chain-3 at beginning of row counts as first double crochet unless otherwise stated.

SPECIAL STITCHES

Shell: (Cl—*see Special Stitches*, ch 3, cl) as indicated in instructions.

Cluster (cl): Holding back last lp of each st on hook, 3 dc as indicated in instructions, yo, pull through all lps on hook.

INSTRUCTIONS

Row 1 (WS): Dc in 4th ch from hook (*first 3 chs count as first dc*), dc in each of next 2 chs, [ch 1, sk next ch, dc in each of next 3 chs], dc in last ch, turn.

Row 2: Ch 3 (*see Pattern Notes*), sk next dc, **shell** (*see Special Stitches*) in next dc, shell in center

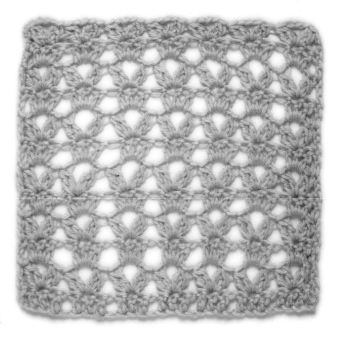

dc of each dc group across, ending with dc in last st, turn.

Row 3: Ch 3, 3 dc in ch sp of next shell, [ch 1, 3 dc in ch sp of next shell] across, dc in last st, turn.

Rep rows 2 and 3 alternately for pattern. ■

#85 This Way & That

PATTERN NOTES

Item shown made with size H/8/5mm crochet hook and Bernat Satin medium (worsted) weight yarn.

Pattern is worked in multiples of 4 plus 8 chains.

Chain-3 at beginning of row counts as first double crochet unless otherwise stated.

INSTRUCTIONS

Row 1 (RS): Dc in 6th ch from hook (*first 5 chs count as first dc and sk 2 chs*), dc in next ch, ch 1, working over last 2 dc, dc in 4th ch, [sk next 2 chs, dc in each of next 2 chs, ch 1, working over last 2 dc, dc in first sk ch] across, ending with dc in last ch, turn.

Row 2: Ch 3 (*see Pattern Notes*), [sk next dc and next ch sp, dc in each of next 2 dc, ch 1,

working over 2 dc just worked, dc in sk dc] across, ending with dc in last st, turn.

Rep row 2 for pattern. ∎

#86 Dip Stitch

PATTERN NOTES

Item shown made with size H/8/5mm crochet hook and Bernat Satin medium (worsted) weight yarn.

Pattern is worked in multiples of 8 plus 11 chains.

Chain-3 at beginning of row counts as first double crochet unless otherwise stated.

INSTRUCTIONS

Row 1 (RS): Dc in 4th ch from hook (*first 3 chs count as first dc*), dc in next ch, *ch 3, sk next 3 chs**, dc in each of next 5 chs, rep from * across, ending last rep at **, dc in each of last 3 chs, turn.

Row 2: Ch 3 (*see Pattern Notes*), dc in each of next 2 dc, *working over next ch-3, 3 dc in center sk ch below**, dc in each of next 5 dc,

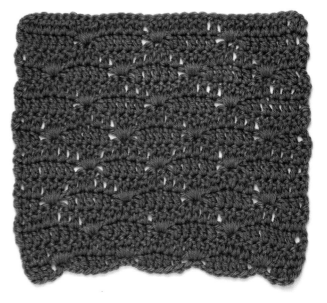

rep from * across, ending last rep at **, dc in each of last 7 dc, turn.

Row 3: Ch 3, dc in each of next 6 dc, *ch 3, sk next 3 dc**, dc in each of next 5 dc, rep from * across, ending last rep at **, dc in each of last 7 dc, turn.

Row 4: Ch 3, dc in each of next 6 dc, [working over next ch-3, 3 dc in center sk st on row before last, dc in each of next 5 dc] across, dc in each of last 2 dc, turn.

Row 5: Ch 3, dc in each of next 2 dc, *ch 3, sk next 3 dc**, dc in each of next 5 dc, rep from *

across, ending last rep at **, dc in each of last 3 dc, turn.

Row 6: Ch 3, dc in each of next 2 dc, *working over next ch-3, 3 dc in center sk dc below**, dc in each of next 5 dc, rep from * across, ending last rep at **, dc in each of last 3 dc, turn.

Rep rows 3–6 consecutively for pattern. ■

#87 Medallion

PATTERN NOTES
Item shown made with size H/8/5mm crochet hook and Bernat Satin medium (worsted) weight yarn.

Pattern is worked in multiples of 7 plus 13 chains.

Chain-3 at beginning of row counts as first double crochet unless otherwise stated.

SPECIAL STITCH
Shell: (3 dc, ch 1, 3 dc) as indicated in instructions.

INSTRUCTIONS
Row 1 (RS): 3 dc in 4th ch from hook (*first 3 chs count as first dc*), [ch 3, sk next 6 chs, **shell** (*see Special Stitch*) in next ch] across to last 8 chs, ch 3, sk next 6 chs, 3 dc in next ch, dc in last ch, turn.

Row 2: Ch 3 (*see Pattern Notes*), 3 dc in next dc, [ch 2, shell in ch sp of next shell] across, ch 2, sk next 2 dc, 3 dc in next dc, dc in last dc, turn.

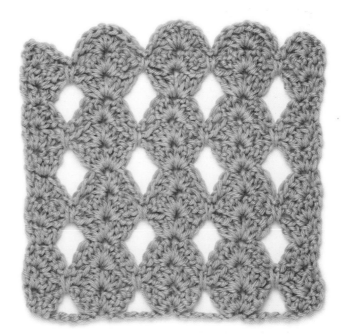

Row 3: Ch 3, 3 dc in next dc, [ch 1, working over ch sp of last row, sc in ch sp on row before last, ch 1, shell in ch sp of next shell] across, ending with ch 1, sk next 2 dc, 3 dc in next dc, dc in last dc, turn.

Row 4: Ch 3, 3 dc in next dc, [ch 2, shell in ch sp of next shell] across, ending with ch 1, sk next 2 dc, 3 dc in next dc, dc in last dc, turn.

Rep rows 2–4 consecutively for pattern. ■

#88 Arched Pillars

PATTERN NOTES
Item shown made with size H/8/5mm crochet hook and Bernat Satin medium (worsted) weight yarn.

Pattern is worked in multiples of 7 plus 10 chains.

Chain-3 at beginning of row counts as first double crochet unless otherwise stated.

SPECIAL STITCH
Shell: 6 dc as indicated in instructions.

INSTRUCTIONS
Row 1 (WS): Dc in 4th ch from hook (*first 3 chs count as first dc*), dc in next ch, *ch 2, sk next 2 chs**, dc in each of next 5 chs, rep from * across, ending last rep at **, dc in each of last 3 chs, turn.

Row 2: **Ch 3** (*see Pattern Notes*), *shell (*see Special Stitch*) in next ch sp, sk next 2 dc**, **fpdc** (*see Stitch Guide*) around next dc, rep from * across, ending last rep at **, dc in last st, turn.

Row 3: Ch 3, dc in each of next 2 dc, *ch 2, dc in each of next 2 dc**, **bpdc** (*see Stitch Guide*) around fpdc, dc in each of next 2 dc, rep from * across, ending last rep at **, dc in last st, turn.

Rep rows 2 and 3 alternately for pattern. ∎

#89 Festive

PATTERN NOTES
Item shown made with size H/8/5mm crochet hook and Bernat Satin medium (worsted) weight yarn.

Pattern is worked in multiples of 6 plus 9 chains.

Chain-3 at beginning of row counts as first double crochet unless otherwise stated.

SPECIAL STITCHES
Shell: (Sc, ch 3, 3 dc) as indicated in instructions.

V-stitch (V-st): (Dc, ch 3, dc) as indicated in instructions.

INSTRUCTIONS

Row 1 (RS): **Shell** (*see Special Stitches*) in 2nd ch from hook, [sk next 6 chs, shell in next ch] across to last 7 chs, sk next 6 chs, sc in last ch, turn.

Row 2: Ch 3 (*see Pattern Notes*), 3 dc in same st as beg ch-3, shell in ch sp of each shell across to last shell, sc in ch sp of last shell, ch 2, dc in last st, turn.

Row 3: Ch 1, sc in first st, [**V-st** (*see Special Stitches*) in next sc, sc in next ch sp] across, ending with sc in last st, turn.

Row 4: Ch 5, sc in next ch sp, [ch 5, sc in next ch sp] across, ending with ch 2, dc in last sc, forming last ch sp, turn.

Row 5: Ch 3, 3 dc in last ch sp formed, shell in each ch sp across, ending with sc in last st, turn.

Rep rows 2–5 consecutively for pattern. ∎

#90 Imagination

PATTERN NOTES

Item shown made with size H/8/5mm crochet hook and Bernat Satin medium (worsted) weight yarn.

Pattern is worked in multiples of 9 plus 8 chains.

Chain-5 at beginning of row counts as first double crochet and chain-2 unless otherwise stated.

INSTRUCTIONS

Row 1 (RS): Dc in 8th ch from hook (*first 7 chs count as first dc, sk 2 chs and ch-2*), [ch 2, sk next 2 chs, dc in next ch] across, turn.

Row 2: Ch 5 (*see Pattern Notes*), dc in next dc, [4 dc in next dc, dc in next dc, ch 2, dc in next dc] across, turn.

Row 3: Ch 5, [dc in each of next 6 dc, ch 2] across, ending with dc in last st, turn.

Row 4: Ch 5, *dc dec (*see Stitch Guide*) in next 3 dc, ch 2, dc dec in next 3 dc**, ch 3, rep from * across, ending last rep at **, ch 2, dc in last st, turn.

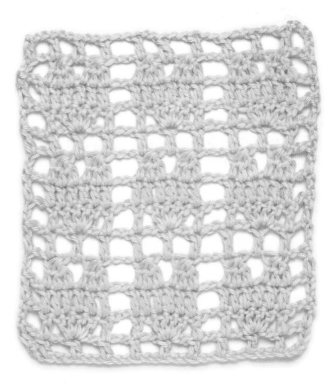

Row 5: Ch 5, [dc in next dc dec, ch 2, dc in next ch-2 sp, ch 2, dc in next dc dec, ch 2] across, dc in last st, turn.

Rep rows 2–5 consecutively for pattern. ∎

#91 Popcorn Squares

PATTERN NOTES
Item shown made with size H/8/5mm crochet
hook and Bernat Satin medium (worsted)
weight yarn.

Pattern is worked in multiples of 8 plus
10 chains.

Chain-3 at beginning of row counts as first
double crochet unless otherwise stated.

Chain-4 at beginning of row counts as
first double crochet and chain-1 unless
otherwise stated.

SPECIAL STITCH
Reverse popcorn (reverse pc): 4 dc as indicated
in instructions, drop lp from hook, insert hook
from back to front in first dc of dc group, pull
dropped lp through.

INSTRUCTIONS
Row 1 (RS): Dc in 4th ch from hook (*first 3 chs
count as first dc*), dc in each of next 5 chs, [ch 1,
dc in each of next 7 chs] across, turn.

Row 2: **Ch 3** (*see Pattern Notes*), dc in each of
next 2 dc, **reverse pc** (*see Special Stitch*) in next
st, dc in each of next 3 dc, [ch 1, dc in each of
next 3 dc, reverse pc, dc in each of next 3 dc]
across, turn.

Row 3: Ch 3, dc in each of next 6 sts, [ch 1, dc in
each of next 7 sts] across, turn.

Row 4: **Ch 4** (*see Pattern Notes*), sk next dc, dc in
next dc, [ch 1, sk next dc or ch sp, dc in next dc]
across, turn.

Row 5: Ch 3, dc in next ch sp, [dc in next st, dc
in next ch sp] twice, dc in next dc, *ch 1, sk next
ch sp, [dc in next dc, dc in next ch sp] 3 times,
dc in next dc, rep from * across, turn.

Rep rows 2–5 consecutively for pattern. ∎

#92 Gentle Waves

PATTERN NOTES

Item shown made with size H/8/5mm crochet
hook and Bernat Satin medium (worsted)
weight yarn.

Pattern is worked in multiples of 8 plus
5 chains.

Chain-3 at beginning of row counts as first
double crochet unless otherwise stated.

SPECIAL STITCH

Shell: (2 dc, ch 1, 2 dc) as indicated in
instructions.

INSTRUCTIONS

Row 1: Dc in 4th ch from hook (*first 3 chs count
as first dc*), dc in next ch, [sk next 2 chs, **shell**
(*see Special Stitch*) in next ch, sk next 2 chs, dc
in each of next 3 chs] across, turn.

Row 2: Ch 3 (*see Pattern Notes*), **fpdc** (*see Stitch
Guide*) around each of next 2 dc, *shell in ch sp
of next shell**, sk all dc of shells, fpdc around
each of next 3 dc, rep from * across, ending last

rep at **, fpdc around each of next 2 dc, dc in
last dc, turn.

Row 3: Ch 3, fpdc around each of next 2 fpdc,
*shell in ch sp of next shell**, fpdc around
next 3 fpdc, rep from * across, ending last rep
at **, fpdc around each of next 2 fpdc, dc in last
dc, turn.

Rep row 3 for pattern. ∎

#93 Composition

PATTERN NOTES

Item shown made with size H/8/5mm crochet
hook and Bernat Satin medium (worsted)
weight yarn.

Pattern is worked in multiples of 6 plus
8 chains.

Chain-3 at beginning of row counts as first
double crochet unless otherwise stated.

INSTRUCTIONS

Row 1 (WS): Sc in 6th ch from hook (*first 5 chs
count as sk 2 chs and ch-3*), [ch 3, sk next 2 chs,
sc in next ch] across to last 2 chs, ch 1, sk next
ch, hdc in last ch, turn.

Row 2: Ch 3 (see Pattern Notes), dc in next ch-1 sp, *ch 3, sc in next ch-3 sp, ch 3**, 3 dc in next ch-3 sp, rep from * across, ending last rep at **, dc in last ch-1 sp, hdc in last st, turn.

Row 3: Ch 3, sc in next ch-3 sp, [ch 3, sc in next ch-3 sp] across, ending with ch 1, hdc in last st, turn.

Rep rows 2 and 3 alternately for pattern. ■

#94 Encounter

PATTERN NOTES
Item shown made with size H/8/5mm crochet hook and Bernat Satin medium (worsted) weight yarn.

Pattern is worked in multiples of 6 plus 8 chains.

Chain-3 at beginning of row counts as first double crochet unless otherwise stated.

Chain-4 at beginning of row counts as first double crochet and chain-1 unless otherwise stated.

INSTRUCTIONS
Row 1: Dc in 4th ch from hook (first 3 chs count as first dc), [ch 3, sk next 3 chs, dc in each of next 3 chs] across to last 5 chs, ch 3, sk next 3 chs, dc in each of last 2 chs, turn.

Row 2: Ch 3 (see Pattern Notes), sc in next dc, *ch 5, sc in next dc**, ch 3, sk next dc, sc in next dc, rep from * across, ending last rep at **, ch 1, hdc in last st, turn.

Row 3: Ch 1, sc in first st, *5 dc in next ch-5 sp**, sc in next ch-3 sp, rep from * across, ending last rep at **, ch 1, hdc in last st, turn.

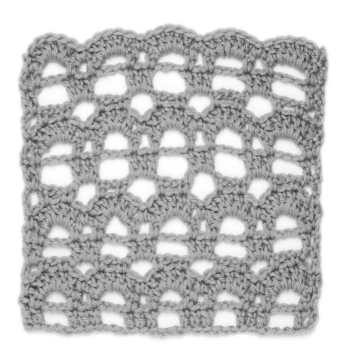

Row 4: Ch 4 (see Pattern Notes), sk next dc, *sc in next dc, ch 1, sk next dc, sc in next dc**, ch 3, sk next 3 sts, rep from * across, ending last rep at **, ch 1, hdc in last st, turn.

Row 5: Ch 3, dc in next ch-1 sp, [ch 3, 3 dc in next ch-3 sp] across, ending with ch 3, dc in each of last 2 sts, turn.

Rep rows 2–5 consecutively for pattern. ■

#95 Flutter

PATTERN NOTES

Item shown made with size H/8/5mm crochet hook and Bernat Satin medium (worsted) weight yarn.

Pattern is worked in multiples of 8 plus 2 chains.

Chain-3 at beginning of row counts as first double crochet unless otherwise stated.

SPECIAL STITCH

Shell: (2 dc, ch 1, dc, ch 1, 2 dc) as indicated in instructions.

INSTRUCTIONS

Row 1 (RS): Sc in 2nd ch from hook, [sk next 3 chs, **shell** (see Special Stitch) in next ch, sk next 3 chs, sc in next ch] across, turn.

Row 2: Ch 3 (see Pattern Notes), [2 dc in next ch-1 sp, ch 1, **bpdc** (see Stitch Guide) around post of next dc, ch 1, 2 dc in next ch-1 sp, dc in next dc] across, turn.

Row 3: Ch 3, [2 dc in next ch-1 sp, ch 1, **fpdc** (see Stitch Guide) around next bpdc, ch 1, 2 dc in next ch-1 sp, dc in next dc] across, turn.

Rep rows 2 and 3 alternately for pattern. ∎

#96 Ridged Clusters

PATTERN NOTES

Item shown made with size H/8/5mm crochet hook and Bernat Satin medium (worsted) weight yarn.

Pattern is worked in multiples of 10 plus 7 chains.

Chain-3 at beginning of row counts as first double crochet unless otherwise stated.

SPECIAL STITCHES

Split decrease (split dec): Holding back last lp of each st on hook, dc in each of next 2 chs, sk next ch, dc in each of next 2 chs, yo, pull through all lps on hook.

Split cluster (split cl): Holding back last lp of each st on hook, 2 dc in next ch-2 sp, sk next split cl, 2 dc in next ch sp, yo, pull through all lps on hook.

INSTRUCTIONS

Row 1: Dc in 4th ch from hook (*first 3 chs count as first dc*), dc in each of next 5 chs, [ch 2, **split dec** (*see Special Stitches*), ch 2, dc in each of next 5 chs] across, turn.

Row 2: Ch 3 (*see Pattern Notes*), **fpdc** (*see Stitch Guide*) around each of next 4 dc, *ch 2, **split cl** (*see Special Stitches*), ch 2**, fpdc around each of next 5 sts, rep from * across, ending last rep at **, fpdc around each of next 4 sts, dc in last st, turn.

Rep row 2 for pattern. ■

#97 Double Doubles

PATTERN NOTES

Item shown made with size H/8/5mm crochet hook and Bernat Satin medium (worsted) weight yarn.

Pattern is worked in multiples of 4 plus 8 chains.

Chain-3 at beginning of row counts as first double crochet unless otherwise stated.

INSTRUCTIONS

Row 1: 2 dc in 5th ch from hook (*first 4 chs count as first dc and sk 2 chs*), [sk next 2 chs, 2 dc in each of next 2 chs] across to last 2 chs, sk next ch, dc in last ch, turn.

Row 2: Ch 3 (*see Pattern Notes*), sk next dc, *2 dc in each of next 2 dc**, sk next 2 dc, rep from *

across, ending last rep at **, ending with sk next st, dc in last st, turn.

Rep row 2 for pattern. ■

#98 Sassy

PATTERN NOTES

Item shown made with size H/8/5mm crochet hook and Bernat Satin medium (worsted) weight yarn.

Pattern is worked in multiples of 6 plus 7 chains.

Chain-3 at beginning of row counts as first double crochet unless otherwise stated.

SPECIAL STITCH

Cluster (cl): Holding back last lp of each st on hook, 2 dc as indicated in instructions, yo, pull through all lps on hook.

INSTRUCTIONS

Row 1 (WS): Sc in 7th ch from hook (*first 6 chs count as first sc, ch-3 and sk 2 chs*), [ch 3, sk next 2 chs, sc in next ch] across, turn.

Row 2 (RS): **Ch 3** (*see Pattern Notes*), *cl (*see Special Stitch*) in next ch sp, ch 1, 3 dc in next ch sp**, ch 1, rep from * across, ending last rep at **, dc in last st, turn.

Row 3: Ch 1, sc in first st, [ch 3, sc in next ch sp] across, ch 3, sc in last st, turn.

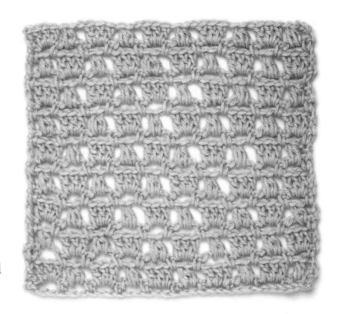

Row 4: Ch 3, *3 dc in next ch sp, ch 1, cl in next ch sp**, ch 1, rep from * across, ending last rep at **, dc in last st, turn.

Row 5: Rep row 3.

Rep rows 2–5 consecutively for pattern. ∎

#99 Funky Shells

PATTERN NOTES

Item shown made with size H/8/5mm crochet hook and Bernat Satin medium (worsted) weight yarn.

Pattern is worked in multiples of 8 plus 2 chains.

Chain-4 at beginning of row counts as first double crochet and chain-1 unless otherwise stated.

SPECIAL STITCHES

Shell: (Dc, {ch 1, dc} 4 times) as indicated in instructions.

Cluster (cl): Holding back last lp of each st on hook, 3 dc as indicated in instructions, yo, pull through all lps on hook.

INSTRUCTIONS

Row 1 (WS): Sc in 2nd ch from hook, [ch 1, sk next 3 chs, **shell** (see Special Stitches) in next ch, ch 1, sk next 3 chs, sc in next ch] across, turn.

Row 2: **Ch 4** (see Pattern Notes), *cl (see Special Stitches) in first ch sp of next shell, ch 2, sc in next ch sp of same shell, ch 1, sc in next ch sp of same shell, ch 2, cl in last ch sp of same shell**, ch 1, rep from * across, ending last rep at **, ch 1, dc in last st, turn.

Row 3: Ch 4, (dc, ch 1, dc) in same st as beg ch-4, *ch 1, sc in next ch-1 sp**, shell in next ch-1 sp, rep from * across, ending last rep at **, ending with (dc, ch 1, 2 dc) in last st, turn.

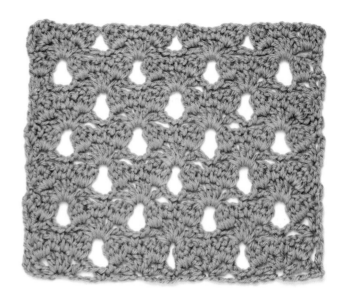

Row 4: Ch 1, sc in first st, sc in next ch-1 sp, cl in next ch-1 sp, ch 1, *cl in first ch-1 sp of next shell, ch 2, sc in next ch-1 sp of same shell, ch 1, sc in next ch sp of same shell, ch 2, cl in next ch sp of same shell, ch 1, sk next 2 ch sps and next sc, rep from * across, cl in next ch-1 sp, ch 1, sc in next ch sp, sc in last st, turn.

Row 5: Ch 1, sc in first st, ch 1, sk next ch sp, [shell in next ch sp, ch 1, sc in next ch sp between sc, ch 1] across, sc in last st, turn.

Rep rows 2–5 consecutively for pattern. ■

#100 Celtic Cross

PATTERN NOTES

Item shown made with size H/8/5mm crochet
hook and Bernat Satin medium (worsted)
weight yarn.

Pattern is worked in multiples of 4 plus
8 chains.

Chain-3 at beginning of row counts as first
double crochet unless otherwise stated.

SPECIAL STITCH

Cluster (cl): Ch 3, dc in 3rd ch from hook.

INSTRUCTIONS

Row 1: Dc in 5th ch from hook (*first 4 chs count
as first dc and sk 1 ch*), *cl (see Special Stitch), sk
next ch**, **dc dec** (*see Stitch Guide*) in next
3 chs, rep from * across, ending last rep at **, dc
dec in last 2 chs, turn.

Row 2: Ch 3 (*see Pattern Notes*), dc in same st
as beg ch-3, ch 1, [dc dec in next 3 sts, ch 1]
across, ending with 2 dc in last st, turn.

Row 3: Ch 2, dc in next st (*ch-2 and last dc
counts as first dc dec*), cl, [3 dc in next dc dec, cl]
across, ending with dc dec in last 2 sts, turn.

Rep rows 2 and 3 alternately for pattern. ∎

Baby Afghan

SKILL LEVEL

EASY

FINISHED MEASUREMENT
36 x 40 inches

MATERIALS
- Bernat Satin medium (worsted) weight acrylic yarn (3½ oz/ 200 yds/100g per skein):
    5 skeins #04420 sea shell
- Size H/8/5mm crochet hook or size needed to obtain gauge

GAUGE
2 pattern reps = 4 inches; 5 pattern rows = 4 inches

PATTERN NOTES
Estimated time: 16½ hours.

Pattern is worked in multiples of 8 plus 12 chains.

Chain-3 at beginning of row counts as first double crochet unless otherwise stated.

Join with slip stitch as indicated unless otherwise stated.

SPECIAL STITCHES
Picot: Ch 3, sl st in top of last dc worked.

Shell: (3 dc, ch 2, 3 dc) as indicated in instructions.

AFGHAN
Row 1 (RS): Ch 140, 3 dc in 4th ch from hook (*first 3 chs count as first dc*), **picot** (*see Special Stitches*), sk next 7 chs, [**shell** (*see Special Stitches*) in next ch, sk next 7 chs] across, ending with 4 dc in last ch, turn. (*16 shells*)

Row 2: **Ch 3** (*see Pattern Notes*), 3 dc in same st as beg ch-3, picot, [shell in ch sp of next shell, picot] across, ending with 4 dc in last st, turn.

Rows 3–50: Rep row 2.

Row 51: Ch 1, sc in first st, [ch 3, sc in next picot, ch 3, sc in ch sp of next shell] across, ending with ch 3, sc in last st. Fasten off.

BORDER
Rnd 1: Working around entire outer edge in sts, ends of rows and in starting ch on opposite side of row 1, with RS facing, join with sc in any corner, sc in same st as beg sc, sc in each dc and each ch-3 sp around with 3 sc in each corner, **join** (*see Pattern Notes*) in beg sc.

Rnd 2: Ch 3, dc in each st around with 3 dc in each center corner st, join in 3rd ch of beg ch-3.

Rnd 3: Ch 3, dc in same st as beg ch 3, [sk next 6 or 7 sts (whichever is necessary to keep work flat), shell in next st, picot] around, ending with 3 dc in same st as beg ch-3, ch 2, join in 3rd ch of beg ch-3. Fasten off. ■

Cozy Throw

SKILL LEVEL
■■□□
EASY

FINISHED MEASUREMENT
39 x 47 inches

MATERIALS
- Medium (worsted) weight acrylic yarn (3½ oz/200 yds/ 100g per skein): 6 skeins of amber
- Size K/10½/6.5mm crochet hook or size needed to obtain gauge

4 MEDIUM

GAUGE
2 pattern reps = 5 inches; 5 pattern rows = 4½ inches

PATTERN NOTES
Estimated time: 24 hours.

Pattern is worked in multiples of 8 plus 12 chains.

By simply using the same pattern and number of stitches required to make the Baby Afghan, you have now increased the width by 3 inches and the length by 7 inches to create a larger overall piece that qualifies as a throw. However, as you can see, the Throw requires 1 additional skein of yarn.

Chain-3 at beginning of row counts as first double crochet unless otherwise stated.

Join with slip stitch as indicated unless otherwise stated.

SPECIAL STITCHES
Picot: Ch 3, sl st in top of last dc worked.

Shell: (3 dc, ch 2, 3 dc) as indicated in instructions.

THROW
Row 1 (RS): Ch 140, 3 dc in 4th ch from hook, **picot** (*see Special Stitches*), sk next 7 chs, [**shell** (*see Special Stitches)* in next ch, sk next 7 chs] across, ending with 4 dc in last ch, turn. (*16 shells*)

Row 2: **Ch 3** (*see Pattern Notes*), 3 dc in same st as beg ch-3, picot, [shell in ch sp of next shell, picot] across, ending with 4 dc in last st, turn.

Rows 3–50: Rep row 2.

Row 51: Ch 1, sc in first st, [ch 3, sc in next picot, ch 3, sc in ch sp of next shell] across, ending with ch 3, sc in last st. Fasten off.

BORDER
Rnd 1: Working around entire outer edge in sts, ends of rows and in starting ch on opposite side of row 1, with RS facing, join with sc in any corner, sc in same st as beg sc, sc in each dc and each ch-3 sp around with 3 sc in each corner, **join** (*see Pattern Notes*) in beg sc.

Rnd 2: Ch 3, dc in each st around with 3 dc in each center corner st, join in 3rd ch of beg ch-3.

Rnd 3: Ch 3, dc in same st as beg ch 3, [sk next 6 or 7 sts (whichever is necessary to keep work flat), shell in next st, picot] around, ending with 3 dc in same st as beg ch-3, ch 2, join in 3rd ch of beg ch-3. Fasten off. ■

Simple Scarves

SKILL LEVEL

EASY

FINISHED MEASUREMENT

6½ x 58 inches

MATERIALS

- Bernat Satin medium (worsted) weight acrylic yarn (3½ oz/ 200 yds/100g per skein): 1 skein for each Scarf
- Sizes H/8/5mm and size M/13/9mm crochet hooks
- Tapestry needle

4 MEDIUM

GAUGE

First row measures 6 inches across.

PATTERN NOTES

Double Doubles on page 78 was used for this pattern.

This Scarf measures 6½ x 58 inches worked in double crochet, using size H hook and five pattern repeats, and takes approximately **six** hours to crochet.

Worked in treble crochet, using a size H hook and five pattern repeats, this Scarf measures 6½ x 58 inches and takes approximately **four** hours to make, two less hours than when worked in single crochet! Increasing the stitch height to treble crochet reduces the time to crochet 33 percent.

Worked in treble crochet, using a size M hook and four pattern repeats, this Scarf also measures 6½ x 58 inches and takes approximately **three and a half hours** to make, two and a half hours less than when worked in single crochet! This method decreases your crochet time 42 percent.

While all three scarves measure the same, the time it takes to make each scarf varies dramatically.

Chain-3 at beginning of row counts as first double crochet unless otherwise stated.

Join with slip stitch as indicated unless otherwise stated.

Chain-4 at beginning of row counts as first treble crochet unless otherwise stated.

SCARF
DOUBLE CROCHET & SIZE H HOOK VERSION

Row 1: Ch 26, 2 dc in 5th ch from hook (*first 4 chs count as first dc and sk 1 ch*), 2 dc in next ch, [sk next 2 chs, 2 dc in each of next 2 chs] across to last 2 chs, sk next ch, dc in last ch, turn.

Row 2: **Ch 3** (*see Pattern Notes*), sk next dc, 2 dc in each of next 2 dc, [sk next 2 dc, 2 dc in each of next 2 dc] across, ending with sk next dc, dc in last dc, turn.

Next rows: Rep row 2 until piece measures 57½ inches.

Last rnd: Working around entire outer edge in sts, ends of rows and in starting ch on opposite side of row 1, ch 1, evenly sp sc around so Scarf lies flat with 3 sc in each corner, **join** (*see Pattern Notes*) in beg sc. Fasten off.

TREBLE CROCHET & SIZE H HOOK VERSION

Row 1: Ch 26, 2 tr in 5th ch from hook (*first 4 chs count as first dc and sk 1 ch*), 2 tr in next ch, [sk next 2 chs, 2 tr in each of next 2 chs] across to last 2 chs, sk next ch, tr in last ch, turn.

This scarf was worked using a size H hook and double crochets.

This scarf was worked
using a size H hook and
treble crochets.

Row 2: Ch 4 (*see Pattern Notes*), sk next tr, 2 tr in each of next 2 tr, [sk next 2 tr, 2 tr in each of next 2 tr] across, ending with sk next tr, dc in last dc, turn.

Next rows: Rep row 2 until piece measures 57½ inches.

Last rnd: Working around entire outer edge in sts, ends of rows and in starting ch on opposite side of row 1, ch 1, evenly sp sc around so Scarf lies flat with 3 sc in each corner, **join** (*see Pattern Notes*) in beg sc. Fasten off.

Sew short ends tog.

TREBLE CROCHET & SIZE M HOOK VERSION

Row 1: Ch 20, 2 tr in 5th ch from hook (*first 4 chs count as first dc and sk 1 ch*), [sk next 2 chs, 2 tr in each of next 2 chs] across to last 3 chs, sk next 2 chs, tr in last ch, turn.

Row 2: Ch 4 (*see Pattern Notes*), sk next tr, 2 tr in each of next 2 tr, [sk next 2 tr, 2 tr in each of next 2 tr] across, ending with sk next tr, dc in last dc, turn.

Next rows: Rep row 2 until piece measures 57½ inches.

Last rnd: Working around entire outer edge in sts, ends of rows and in starting ch on opposite side of row 1, ch 1, evenly sp sc around so Scarf lies flat with 3 sc in each corner, **join** (*see Pattern Notes*) in beg sc. Fasten off.

Sew short ends tog. ∎

This scarf was worked using a size M hook and treble crochets.

STITCH GUIDE

FOR MORE COMPLETE INFORMATION,
VISIT ANNIESCATALOG.COM/STITCHGUIDE

STITCH ABBREVIATIONS

beg	begin/begins/beginning
bpdc	back post double crochet
bpsc	back post single crochet
bptr	back post treble crochet
CC	contrasting color
ch(s)	chain(s)
ch-	refers to chain or space previously made (i.e., ch-1 space)
ch sp(s)	chain space(s)
cl(s)	cluster(s)
cm	centimeter(s)
dc	double crochet (singular/plural)
dc dec	double crochet 2 or more stitches together, as indicated
dec	decrease/decreases/decreasing
dtr	double treble crochet
ext	extended
fpdc	front post double crochet
fpsc	front post single crochet
fptr	front post treble crochet
g	gram(s)
hdc	half double crochet
hdc dec	half double crochet 2 or more stitches together, as indicated
inc	increase/increases/increasing
lp(s)	loop(s)
MC	main color
mm	millimeter(s)
oz	ounce(s)
pc	popcorn(s)
rem	remain/remains/remaining
rep(s)	repeat(s)
rnd(s)	round(s)
RS	right side
sc	single crochet (singular/plural)
sc dec	single crochet 2 or more stitches together, as indicated
sk	skip/skipped/skipping
sl st(s)	slip stitch(es)
sp(s)	space(s)/spaced
st(s)	stitch(es)
tog	together
tr	treble crochet
trtr	triple treble
WS	wrong side
yd(s)	yard(s)
yo	yarn over

YARN CONVERSION

OUNCES TO GRAMS	GRAMS TO OUNCES
1 .... 28.4	25 .... ⅞
2 .... 56.7	40 .... 1⅔
3 .... 85.0	50 .... 1¾
4 .... 113.4	100 .... 3½

UNITED STATES		UNITED KINGDOM
sl st (slip stitch)	=	sc (single crochet)
sc (single crochet)	=	dc (double crochet)
hdc (half double crochet)	=	htr (half treble crochet)
dc (double crochet)	=	tr (treble crochet)
tr (treble crochet)	=	dtr (double treble crochet)
dtr (double treble crochet)	=	ttr (triple treble crochet)
skip	=	miss

Single crochet decrease (sc dec): (Insert hook, yo, draw lp through) in each of the sts indicated, yo, draw through all lps on hook.

Example of 2-sc dec

Half double crochet decrease (hdc dec): (Yo, insert hook, yo, draw lp through) in each of the sts indicated, yo, draw through all lps on hook.

Example of 2-hdc dec

Reverse single crochet (reverse sc): Ch 1, sk first st, working from left to right, insert hook in next st from front to back, draw up lp on hook, yo and draw through both lps on hook.

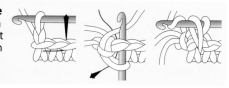

Chain (ch): Yo, pull through lp on hook.

Single crochet (sc): Insert hook in st, yo, pull through st, yo, pull through both lps on hook.

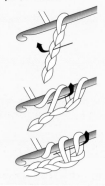

Double crochet (dc): Yo, insert hook in st, yo, pull through st, [yo, pull through 2 lps] twice.

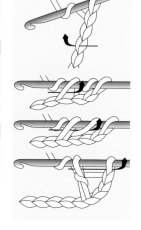

Double crochet decrease (dc dec): (Yo, insert hook, yo, draw lp through, yo, draw through 2 lps on hook) in each of the sts indicated, yo, draw through all lps on hook.

Example of 2-dc dec

Front loop (front lp) Back loop (back lp)

Front Loop   Back Loop

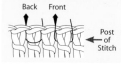

Front post stitch (fp): Back post stitch (bp): When working post st, insert hook from right to left around post of st on previous row.

Back   Front

Post of Stitch

Half double crochet (hdc): Yo, insert hook in st, yo, pull through st, yo, pull through all 3 lps on hook.

Double treble crochet (dtr): Yo 3 times, insert hook in st, yo, pull through st, [yo, pull through 2 lps] 4 times.

Treble crochet decrease (tr dec): Holding back last lp of each st, tr in each of the sts indicated, yo, pull through all lps on hook.

Example of 2-tr dec

Slip stitch (sl st): Insert hook in st, pull through both lps on hook.

Chain color change (ch color change) Yo with new color, draw through last lp on hook.

Double crochet color change (dc color change) Drop first color, yo with new color, draw through last 2 lps of st.

Treble crochet (tr): Yo twice, insert hook in st, yo, pull through st, [yo, pull through 2 lps] 3 times.

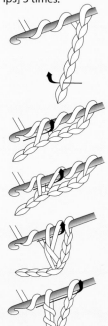

Metric
Conversion
Charts

INCHES INTO MILLIMETRES & CENTIMETRES (Rounded off slightly)

inches	mm	cm	inches	cm	inches	cm	inches	cm
1/8	3	0.3	5	12.5	21	53.5	38	96.5
1/4	6	0.6	5 1/2	14	22	56	39	99
3/8	10	1	6	15	23	58.5	40	101.5
1/2	13	1.3	7	18	24	61	41	104
5/8	15	1.5	8	20.5	25	63.5	42	106.5
3/4	20	2	9	23	26	66	43	109
7/8	22	2.2	10	25.5	27	68.5	44	112
1	25	2.5	11	28	28	71	45	114.5
1 1/4	32	3.2	12	30.5	29	73.5	46	117
1 1/2	38	3.8	13	33	30	76	47	119.5
1 3/4	45	4.5	14	35.5	31	79	48	122
2	50	5	15	38	32	81.5	49	124.5
2 1/2	65	6.5	16	40.5	33	84	50	127
3	75	7.5	17	43	34	86.5		
3 1/2	90	9	18	46	35	89		
4	100	10	19	48.5	36	91.5		
4 1/2	115	11.5	20	51	37	94		

METRIC CONVERSIONS

yards	x	.9144	=	metres (m)
yards	x	91.44	=	centimetres (cm)
inches	x	2.54	=	centimetres (cm)
inches	x	25.40	=	millimetres (mm)
inches	x	.0254	=	metres (m)

centimetres	x	.3937	=	inches
metres	x	1.0936	=	yards

KNITTING NEEDLES CONVERSION CHART

Canada/U.S.	0	1	2	3	4	5	6	7	8	9	10	10½	11	13	15
Metric (mm)	2	2¼	2¾	3¼	3½	3¾	4	4½	5	5½	6	6½	8	9	10

CROCHET HOOKS CONVERSION CHART

Canada/U.S.	1/B	2/C	3/D	4/E	5/F	6/G	8/H	9/I	10/J	10½/K	N
Metric (mm)	2.25	2.75	3.25	3.5	3.75	4.25	5	5.5	6	6.5	9.0

Annie's ® *100 Quick & Easy Crochet Stitches* is published by Annie's, 306 East Parr Road, Berne, IN 46711. Printed in USA. Copyright © 2013 Annie's. All rights reserved. This publication may not be reproduced in part or in whole without written permission from the publisher.

RETAIL STORES: If you would like to carry this pattern book or any other Annie's publication, visit AnniesWSL.com

Every effort has been made to ensure that the instructions in this pattern book are complete and accurate. We cannot, however, take responsibility for human error, typographical mistakes or variations in individual work. Please visit AnniesCustomerCare.com to check for pattern updates.

ISBN: 978-1-59635-794-5
1 2 3 4 5 6 7 8 9